Notes on Literature, Film, and Jazz

Howard Eiland

Spuyten Duyvil
New York City

Earlier versions were published as follows:

"Jazz Notes," *Shuffle Boil* (Winter 2003), 3-9.
"Notes on Film," *Telos* (Spring 2005), 141-164.
"Notes on Eric Dolphy," *Shuffle Boil* (Summer 2006), 21-29.
"Allegories of Falling," *Telos* (Summer 2011), 175-190.
"Steve Lacy: All in the Cooking," *Amerarcana/Shuffle Boil* (October 2016), 27-31.

© 2019 Howard Eiland
ISBN 978-1-949966-02-2

Library of Congress Cataloging-in-Publication Data

Names: Eiland, Howard, author.
Title: Notes on literature, film, and jazz / Howard Eiland.
Description: New York City : Spuyten Duyvil, [2019] | Includes
  bibliographical references.
Identifiers: LCCN 2018053141 | ISBN 9781949966022
Subjects: LCSH: Literature--History and criticism. | Motion
  pictures--History. | Jazz--History and criticism.
Classification: LCC PN511 .E423 2019 | DDC 809--dc23
LC record available at https://lccn.loc.gov/2018053141

A profound reserve of knowledge and wisdom underlies these short, concentrated essays and "notes" about literature, film, and jazz. Each art demands its own vocabulary, but the virtues of Howard Eiland's book are consistent: sharply focused evocations of the works along with sturdy, thought-provoking generalizations; metaphors that help us recognize the humanity in formal features; contrasts that clarify and refine; a vivid and discriminating language for the nonverbal. The reader joins a mind always in motion, probing, questioning, and rethinking. What Eiland says of Herbie Nichols applies equally here: one experiences "doors suddenly opening, one after another."
BONNIE COSTELLO

There is wisdom, grace, beauty, and charm in this handsome little book, whether the subject is Dickens, Shakespeare, and Kafka, or an expanse of twentieth-century cinema, or virtuoso instrumentalists such as Eric Dolphy, Steve Lacy, and Thelonious Monk. This is the kind of book one can love.
STEVE LIGHT

Eiland demonstrates remarkable understanding of the inner workings of literature, film and jazz. His *Notes on Literature* suggest visceral and metaphysical dimensions, while he analyzes brilliantly the plastic language of film and modern jazz.
JUDITH WECHSLER

Eiland's observations about the originality of Herbie Nichols' and Steve Lacy's improvisations are as enlightening as music criticism can get. Whether he is writing about literature, film, or music, Eiland's wit, learning, and daring continuously challenge one's received ideas.
LOUIS KAMPF

for Julia

NOTES ON LITERATURE
   —ELIZABETH AND DARCY   1
   —ALLEGORIES OF FALLING   5

NOTES ON FILM   33

NOTES ON JAZZ
   —ERIC DOLPHY   79
   —STEVE LACY   91
   —PEE WEE RUSSELL   101
   —BEBOP PIANO   102

Notes On Literature

Elizabeth and Darcy

She hardly knew how to suppose she could be an object of admiration to so great a man. Hardly knew. But that was enough. That was a starter. The rest is vengeance—and witchcraft...

Without quite *knowing* what she is doing, at the mercy of her vanity and darker instincts while bravely seeking to realize her ideals, Elizabeth Bennet somewhat quixotically enters into battle. For the sake of her cherished vision of marriage, which imperils her material security and that of her family, she takes aim at that cocky young man leaning against the mantlepiece, battling to make the gentleman truly gentle—and thus to bring about the marriage of happiness and justice.

She teaches him to play and that is their salvation. It is intellectual seduction.

She tells him, late in their courtship: You must always respect and praise me, and in return it belongs to me to torment you whenever I please. You're the man, after all, and, according to your own philosophy, must suffer. Her speech seems playfully to echo the exalted beloved of courtly romance, and behind that the fierce archaic goddess who exacts sacrifices. Think of Penelope testing Odysseus. In her freedom from the patriarchal myth (something doubtless conditioned on her warm and *honest* relationship with her father, no tower of strength), Elizabeth can appropriate the myth, or rather make salutary experimental use of it, satirizing her own progressivism and hence legitimating it in the face of unreflecting and oppressive feudal legacies and resurgent mythic powers, Lady Catherine breathing fire, the darker nature infusing the comedy of sacred matrimony. Satire as vigilance.

It is their determination to know—it is, in short, the courage to interrogate themselves—that first turns the battle into play, that *civilizes* it. He could leave after her formal reply, which parodies his establishmentarianism, but he chooses to stay and run the gauntlet, seeking to discover her reason for rejecting his proposal (just as she will persevere in reading the letter that occasions her own mortification). And this is all she needs to really let him have it. He takes it—as she perhaps knew he would—in the mutually educative violence of discovery.

A climactic moment in a long tradition going back through Molière, Shakespeare, and Chaucer to Aristophanes. After this, the battle of the sexes would never be the same.

Jane Austen is plenty revolutionary when it comes to "family values." The family in her novels is generally the site of the most disastrous failures of education, and family squabbling is seen as almost the greatest of evils.

Austen has in common with Kant (who taught that the human being becomes human solely through education) the capacity to think from out of the sensuous and the intelligible—"affection" and "conviction"—at one and the same time. Utopian vision married to sober realism. One could speak of her critical idealism.

Utopian vision) marriage as dialectic in action: the "man" is for abstract principle but follows his heart, incurring some danger, while the "woman" defends pliant friendship but strives to do what is right, placing principle above self-interest.

Sober realism) marriage as solace for neither mind nor body: Mrs Bennet is all too familiar to the husband who has lived with her these three and twenty years, while Mr Bennet remains a distant and essentially unknown figure in his wife's daily life.

What the first scene of *Pride and Prejudice* establishes is that there is generally no real civility in marriage. What Elizabeth (like Beatrice and the Wife of Bath) demands and finally gets in matrimony, although only after dire struggle with *herself*, is the highest civility.

At its most ambiguous development toward the end, however, the text invites a cynical reading of things: namely, that Elizabeth has made use of arts and allurements to secure an exceedingly comfortable marriage for herself, while Darcy by his latest intervention has bought her love, securing her gratitude to him more effectively than Mr Collins could ever have done.

Very significant, of course, that Darcy's first proposal takes place in Collins's house, where marriage is very much a calculated business affair. The sound of the door shutting conclusively at the scene's end—masterful touch—springs her tears from some deep and confused well of feeling within. They are not yet in the open, morally speaking, but still hedged round by ancient precedent, their grand experiment waiting to be born.

In a modern perspective, Elizabeth Bennet is the defender of individualistic democratic values against feudal dogma and dynasticism. In a classical perspective, she is the fairest blossom of English womanhood, and

Mr Darcy must fully waken to the responsibility of stewardship. In either case, there is transcendence of external and internal power relations between persons.

The visit to Pemberley: redemption after mutual mortification. Quite unexpectedly—and the sudden break in routine time and space is subtly indicative—they experience a new consideration for each other, prelude to tenderness, as they walk outdoors, into the open, equal partners in adventure. For the first time they are thoughtfully silent with each other, conscious of their mutual gratitude and mutual shame beyond all difference of background, and hardly able, in the barely acknowledged consummation of the moment, to remember where they are, although Elizabeth is still capable of casting a sly look his way when she introduces her genteel and amiable companions as—will he bear the blow?—her *relatives*, half expecting him now to decamp from the field of battle with his followers. But his exceedingly civil and—mirabile dictu—almost shy invitation to meet his own dearest relative leaves her, at visit's end, as her happily married aunt and uncle look on and gently tease, feeling only wonder.

So what then do we make of "sexual difference" (the very term is equivocal)? Austen, it may be said, has a more virile mind than Dickens. — Falling in love is for her protagonists a temptation to be avoided or overcome in the interests of true friendship, which is something one builds over time on a foundation of respect rather than falls into.

Allegories of Falling

And therefore as a stranger give it welcome...

At the end, in a role-reversal at once desperate and sublime, Hamlet stills the unaccustomed passion of his stoical friend Horatio by reminding him he's a man first, before being a Dane or antique Roman. He recalls him to himself out of his suicidal flurry by simultaneously appealing to his love and assigning him a duty: in this harsh world to remain and "tell my story"—an echo of the parting words of his father's spirit near the beginning of the play ("Remember me"). Hamlet has now become the ghost.

"I am dead, Horatio…" I am *as* dead. A final equivocation in view of the ineradicable complicity of being and semblance. To adapt a suggestion by Coleridge: Hamlet looks on things as if they were already past.[1] He sees the world from the perspective of the dead.

"What is a man…?" He alludes to the old enigma in the face of his own burgeoning shame and the visitations of the spirit, knowing himself to be more than a little lower than the angels—in a just accounting, no one would "scape whipping"—and less certain of enlightenment than the psalmist who asked what man is. In putting on an antic disposition as a personal and

---

1 "Hamlet beheld external things in the same way that a man of vivid imagination, who shuts his eyes, sees what has previously made an impression on his organs." Coleridge argues that the world for Hamlet is dim and insubstantial where it is not reflected in the mirror of his mind (*Lectures of 1811-1812*, Lecture XII).

political stratagem, while unraveling, anatomizing, and experimentally liquidating his own identity, or the received idea of his identity, he becomes who he is—the melancholic questioner himself the chief question—and articulates the riddle of human fate: to be *and* not to be. The duty to remember is predicated on this equivocation in being.

Contrast "I am dead" with the villain's "I am but hurt" and his fruitless appeal to "friends." Everyone at court, and Claudius above all, recognizes Hamlet's innate nobility: the compound of a generous, uncalculating nature and "something dangerous." When the ghost first waves him on to a ground more removed, in proximity to the cliff and the flood, he unhesitatingly puts knowledge before safety, his frank maidenly soul being presumed immortal: "I do not set my life at a pin's fee." What in Claudius's eyes is, revealingly, "unmanly grief" coexists in Hamlet's nature with a philosophical soldierliness as well as with a philosophical playfulness.

This chance,[2] this act: "You that look pale and tremble at this chance, / That are but mutes or audience to this act." The play's central problematic—that of *play* itself—is concentrated in these stock phrases. The player, in a fiction, generates real emotions; the tendered artifice—"the bait of falsehood"—draws out the hidden truth. The actor becomes the man of action, and precisely by virtue of his improvisation of himself at the bidding of necessity, in the midst of crisis, an enterprise at once political, moral, and religious. Hence, for one who makes the dramatic "interim" his own, the play's the *thing*—the

---

[2] Meaning literally what falls, like dice or dying bodies, what befalls (*cadentia*).

deciding public thing in the old sense of the word—and the stage is the arena. What eventuates is a game of hazard, a deadly serious theatrical, in which affairs of state are seen to turn on "actions that a man might play." Authority is put to the test and justified only insofar as it is truly ventured and made to suffer a sea change. Having "by indirections" passed through the aporias of reason and, as a consequence of the most circumspect analysis, traversed the gap between argument and deed, having gazed long into the abyssal mirror of self-consciousness and witnessed the transformation of philosophy in the reflection of nothingness—that looming grave—when honor's at the stake, Hamlet can resolutely "fall to play," as Claudius and Fortinbras in different ways have done before him. Attacking the intractable problem of revenge (the problem of evil) from a multitude of angles, he readies himself for an opening in the tightening mesh of circumstances, and at the critical moment, without having resolved the problem rationally, he leaps. The strange mordant mood of the graveyard scene, in which the Prince plays straight man to the Gravedigger and looks into the future of his "own" body ("Whose grave's this?"), is the prelude to a culminating vision of world play and existential wager, a new and essentially ambiguous dance of death. The detail of the "mountebank" from whom Laertes purchases poison confirms the note of witchcraft festivity, previously introduced in the performance of *The Mousetrap*, when the Player-Murderer, under the spell of "Hecate's ban," applies his midnight weeds to "poison in jest," whereupon the wholesome garden grows rank. The mention of the famed "Lamord" toward the end—"this gallant had witchcraft in't"—belongs in this context. The allegory *plays* like a dream.

Hamlet makes use of semblance in order to be. This is symptomatic of what Plato calls the rare growth of a philosophical mind. For truth has its incarnation in mimesis, a mutable world of seeming, plump fruit of nonbeing. Except that Hamlet's education—as archetypally modern—is a movement into, rather than out of, the cave of shadows. He does not abandon godlike reason but dismantles and dismembers it, bringing into view its dynamic basis in time and language ("such large discourse looking before and after"). To find quarrel in a straw—words, words, words—is to introduce an oceanic principle into thinking. Fundamentally strange to himself, Hamlet welcomes the strange and finally puts himself into the enemy's hands in order to deal with him.

The spirit of dance that governs comedy in the name of an all-encompassing generative eros is ruptured in tragedy, where it assumes a disjointed or blasted form in the "ecstasy" of sacrifice.

Shakespeare's cogito, spoken by King Lear in the mode of a question, as he seeks some perspective on his situation: "Who is it that can tell me who I am?" (an echo and elaboration of the opening line of *Hamlet*: "Who's there?"). The answer, "Lear's shadow," spoken by the Fool, goes beyond Descartes in its feeling for the interfusion of opposites—wisdom and folly, light and darkness, sound and silence, self and other. King Lear recognizes and realizes himself, embracing the fullest responsibility for his kingdom, the highest and widest justice, when he becomes the shadow of himself and enters the realm of shadow—the realm of night, storm, sea, and madness. When he winds up beside himself, in philosophic free fall, and unlearns who he is. He thereby divests his earthly existence of all certainty in worldly accommodation and exposes himself to the "nothing" he has so rashly invoked, as Hamlet invokes the being of nonbeing. They are both in varying degrees distracted, Hamlet and Lear, both estranged from their former expectations of order, although, as true individual consciences of their respective polities, they are equally independent of established authority and equally grounded in the groundless. Each incarnates a higher, more dangerous and more rigorous, unaccommodated authority.

If *Hamlet* is about knowledge, *Lear* is about love... When Gloucester at the beginning asks lightly, "Do you smell a fault?"—it is of course the "sulphurous pit" that is at issue. The whoremaster is conceived in joy and born in shame, a monster of the deep. Hamlet too is obsessed with bad smells, organic and otherwise. Even reason may "fust in us unused" (in us as individuals, or as a nation) and become the rotting corpse of itself.

In its Gothicism—one might say, Gothic Christianity—*King Lear* oscillates between the terrors of the earth and the unpublished virtues of the earth. Its thematic trajectory turns on an idea of nakedness or vulnerability, as entry: "We came crying hither..." Likewise Hamlet, sea-changed, tells Claudius that he is "set naked" on his kingdom. Losing oneself to find oneself: such immersion in the elemental—as intimately allied to the capacity for grieving—is the precondition for kingship no less than for love.

Lear *knows* he retains in his very person a necessarily imperiled authority, but he *learns* that his singularity is bound up with mortal folly, with all that is common. It is the wise Fool who distinguishes between knowing and learning ("Learn more than thou trowest").

Truth must be whipped out, the Fool says, must be felt on the skin and in the heart. One must pass beyond the firmly established, conventional "marks of sovereignty, knowledge, and reason," eschewing "roofs" both physical and metaphysical, if one is ever to assay the primordial nakedness of truth. It is nothing one can possess or signify, nothing had or known, though it is perhaps sensed—as a certain unfathomable gravity. It is and is not at hand: "No cause, no cause."

Lear learns what he needs to know—about loving the child as a gift and not a disposable property, much less a sop to his vanity—and having ceased his ranting about the ingratitude of children, having become in the end a king of nothing, the human being as God's spy, he fixes his gaze on what is forever lost and, shattered but unvanquished, obedient only to the imponderable "weight of this sad time," sinks to the earth. In her stern, almost vindictive grace, Cordelia likewise has renounced the seemly and the prudent—what Hamlet calls the uses of this world, as opposed to that within which passes show—and, in defense of the unwritten rights of love, has worked to teach her father a lesson about gratitude and true need. About radical imperfection of the heart.

The Fool, the Gravedigger, the irrepressible bawdy: the note of the absurd lightens the moment while darkening the horizon. Don Quixote, who learns nothing except perhaps that he is mad, and whose madness erupts in the name of justice, is the obverse of King Lear. Like the satyr Socrates, who leaves his disciples with the darkest of jokes—"I owe a cock to Asclepius"—these figures of unraveled reason ultimately take us beyond the distinction between tragedy and comedy. (We may imagine that, on some level, Lear *wants* to abandon hearth and home and go wandering.)

***

Pip's fruition: the ripening of a prodigal heart in the soil of remorse. For all his ebullience and whimsicality, Dickens never lost sight of what he called the old wild violent nature and the constant imminence of engulfment. His most perfect novel begins with the protagonist's first impression of the identity of things, which is at once vivid and broad. The focus expands outward—past graveyard, marshes, and river, to the sea, the furthest imaginable limit embodying the origin of things—before suddenly concentrating inward, to the trembling center: the child sitting with the dead. We must go out into the world in order to find the self, and such navigation of the "winds and waves" is in principle a return home—to original sin. We come (back) to ourselves from out of the other, remembering who we must be in the face of all we have lost, all oblivious assimilation to the "vast engine clashing and whirling over a gulf."

Pip truly enters the world when he turns back to that ground from which so many ghosts have started, when he finally embraces his past, with its manifold untoward claims. In writing down the story of his own life, he wakes from and to the dream of what has been. He breaks the spell of an imagined future and thereby discovers the previously hidden *meaning* of the past. The mists gradually rise as the truth is unearthed, although the nameless shadow remains to envelop the small circle of light. His expectations were a kind of bottomless delirium. Having confounded impossible existences with his own identity, and having glimpsed through the torn veil of his romantic delusions the maelstrom within, he hearkens at last to the "old home-voice" of his earliest protector and only true parent, the blacksmith Gargery, who, while never assuming any overt authority over the orphan he saved from want, has quietly taught him how to live by instilling a conscience.

Just as quietly, the ocean, the earth, and the sky frame the opening of *Great Expectations*, putting all the social drama in perspective.

Miss Havisham stands at the opposite extreme from Mr. Jaggers, with respect to time and money. She is all pathos where he is irony. Joe Gargery mediates between these extremes—he lives and works in a present imbued with the past (the old ways of the forge, the memory of the "little child")—and is thus, in his elemental strength and gentleness, his utterly nontyrannical authority that gives the appearance of foolishness, the moral touchstone for Pip's personal retrospection and mature analysis of society. At the end, the extremes meet. Jaggers fleetingly acknowledges the claim of dreams, and the disheveled old waxwork witch becomes the exemplar of sanity and decency, in all her bitter broken-heartedness and distraction.

She spontaneously combusts at the end; it is no mischance. Her heart is rudely awakened from its long stony sleep, her humanity momentarily restored, as she encounters a reflection of her former doomed love in Pip's passion for Estella. But she succumbs very quickly to the return of the repressed, intensified now to the point of explosion, and is consumed along with her train of ghosts. As Pip learns from his own harsh experience, the past once estranged will have its revenges.

The various and often subtle references to *Hamlet* in the novel are not incidental. Despite the partly comic context (Mr. Wopsle's fusty but feeling performance as the Dane in London), they serve to augment the prevailing melancholy. The bleak churchyard depicted at the beginning, recalling the spot where Hamlet comes down to earth after being at sea, is the gravitational center of Pip's existence and of the novel's action. It forms a pendant to the ruined garden of Satis House, which, like the rank, unweeded garden to which Hamlet compares the world, betokens not only lack of stewardship but violated innocence and the unruly growth of self-consciousness over time. In the churchyard appears the ghost of the father—Magwitch will become like a father to Pip— and it is from that fatal, inescapable apparition that the profoundly indecisive hero, awash in the depths of his own imagination and memory, draws inspiration to come of age and to realize himself in sacrifice. To father himself, as Stephen Dedalus puts it. The hero is here a bachelor, a "maid," who must learn to swim in the corrupted currents of this world; the sea is evoked in both works to mark the shadowy entry into adulthood, as prepared by a certain renunciation. Bentley Drummle is Pip's phallic double (phallic and "brutal"), as Claudius is Hamlet's. The struggling lost soul of man is redeemed only after the ideal of purity is simultaneously relaxed and tempered in exposure to evil.

Hamlet's question, the question of being and nonbeing, nobility and freedom, presupposes an idea of the human as something more—but also something less—than the hungry, vigilant animal ensnared and fulfilled in the immediate present, presupposes a capacity for "looking before and after," that is, living in a stratified depth of time defined by remembering and imagining. Freedom is this rooted spanning, this capacity to *err*—spirit of play reverberating necessities of the heart. Both Hamlet and Pip grow in readiness, the player's virtue. They learn to wait for the opening and to take the cue, which may come like a thief in the night. Ultimately, their experience of a destructive saving "providence"—Magwitch's assumed name is "Provis"—obliterates the difference between active and receptive, or action and contemplation, and turns life into story.

Pip and Ivan Ilych—in their different ways exemplifying "that within which passes show"—both learn through suffering, through experience in which life and death converge, that the customary grounds of existence are a makeshift, that truth is a black hole into which we fall at every moment, whether we realize it or not, and that all we can fairly do in negotiating the fall, once we have come to know it in the flesh, is to serve others, to grieve for them, and to ask forgiveness. Their stories constitute a standard by which to measure claims of human progress.

***

For Kafka, the expulsion from Paradise is an ongoing affair, is constantly being reenacted in history and the moral life. We are falling anew at every second. Although the expulsion is final and life in the world unavoidable, the eternal recurrence of a lapse from grace makes it possible, he suggests in a series of short idiosyncratic meditations from the period 1917-1918,[3] that we are in some sense still in Paradise, however hard it is to recognize this paradisiacal residence here in the world, where sin is always at the door and man at bottom "an immense swamp." The fact that in ourselves we are able to suffer along with the suffering around us points to the presence of something transcendent, indestructible, in each and all, ramifications of the unknown Tree of Life throughout the deceptive phenomena—or, as he says, property-relations—of Knowledge.

Kafka envisions an entrance to the Holy of Holies in

---

[3] Penned soon after he was first diagnosed with tuberculosis, these short texts were subsequently revised and organized in a numbered sequence of aphorisms to which Max Brod later gave the somewhat misleading title, "Reflections on Sin, Suffering, Hope, and the True Way." Known today as "The Zürau Aphorisms," they form part of *The Blue Octavo Notebooks* (trans. Ernst Kaiser and Eithne Wilkins [Cambridge, MA: Exact Change, 1991]); it is from the latter, unless otherwise indicated, that all Kafka quotations here are taken.

which one takes off not only one's shoes and traveling garment but absolutely everything. One sheds even one's nakedness and what is underneath that, the glimmer (*Schein*) of the undying fire, until in the end there is only the fire itself to be absorbed.

With the fall into knowledge and the mortal world of things is born the possibility of art as unconcealment or at least "dazzlement" of truth. Art, remarks Kafka, is predicated on a certain going astray within the framework of the world. The impenetrable, receding face of truth can be fleetingly illuminated, if at all, only by a kind of lie. It can be caught only in a mirror darkly, glancingly, parabolically. Art flits about the truth with the intention of not getting burned. The answer goes prowling in proximity to the question, follows in desperate pursuit of it along paths leading inevitably away from the answer itself: this is the logic of Kafka's most characteristic narratives. Art as infinite veering en route to the inexplicable.

The Fall is simply the state of sin in which we live, irrespective of any specific guilt. Human being is transgression, is always already errant and astray. Original sin means, among other things, that life is a constant distraction, distracting us even from our distractedness.

Given this conception of the Fall as the determining condition of everyday life and its incurable diaspora, writing becomes a form of prayer, a self-consuming and therefore self-preserving gravitation and gathering of attention in the midst of dispersion. In this way the serpent bites its own tail.

In a fragment, Kafka's narrator sees a snake raise its delicate head out of the large ink bottle into which he is about to dip his pen. Very likely poisonous, he thinks, as he watches it darting its tongue. Writing as intimate descent to the dark powers.

Formula for a nihilistic messianism: The messiah will come only when the most unbridled individualism reigns in matters of the spirit. That is, the messiah will come only when no longer necessary, only after having already arrived.

Ultimate liberation and unending captivity were never mutually exclusive for Kafka. Sorrow and joy, guilt and innocence, were like two indissolubly clasped hands belonging to a single body of flesh and blood. Repugnance for antitheses.

From the diaries: "It is entirely conceivable that life's splendor forever lies in wait about each one of us in all its fullness, but veiled from view, deep down... It *is* there, though, not hostile, not reluctant, not deaf. If you summon it by the right word...it will come" (October 18, 1921). In a world where everything is filled with signs and yet inscrutable, the invocation of a deep-lying fullness of meaning bespeaks an acute sense of the banal.

Kafka, whose face had a boyish look virtually to the last, once defined youth as the ability to perceive beauty. Anyone who retains this ability through life never grows old. But, as he reportedly commented to Gustav Janouch, "we Jews are born old."

Tempted on all sides by recipes for happiness, we have entered a maze of distorting mirrors in which are finally reflected only our greed and vanity: we fall through the mirrors as through trap-doors (comment to Janouch). In other words, the Fall dissimulates itself.

In a diary entry from December 26, 1910, Kafka

speaks of the bountiful transformative power of solitude: "My interior dissolves...and is ready to release what lies deeper." At other times he was inwardly turning to stone, and prodigious efforts were required to shake himself loose, break through the encrusted surface of consciousness, and begin the salutary and demanding immersion: "You have to dive down, as it were, and sink more rapidly than that which sinks in advance of you" (January 30, 1915). What he called self-knowledge was always something precipitous, manifoldly bedeviled, inimical to self-complacence. It found expression in the writing that had its center of gravity in the watery deep.

The reality of the body in Judaism. Kafka's conscious affinity with Kierkegaard did not prevent him from criticizing the latter's separation of the aesthetic from the ethical; there could be no either-or for him in this regard. What counted, what determined life, was the incarnate moment of experience in its summons to witness, a certain vigilant humility *both* aesthetic and ethical. He could therefore represent the Jewish Christ (in conversation with Gustav Janouch) as "an abyss filled with light."

"Sometimes I believe I understand the Fall of Man as no one else" (from a letter of August 13, 1920, to Milena Jesenská). This was no boast, nor confession. In his own eyes, he was the most fortunate and unfortunate of men. He considered himself at once more vulnerable and more heartless, purer and filthier, than other persons, at the same time that he claimed to admire and even envy everyone he met. Without the slightest trace of either self-pity or vanity, he wrote in his diary of the spiritual advantages of despair: anyone who cannot come to terms with the life he is living may nevertheless, in all estrangement, note down what he sees "among the ruins, for he sees different (and more) things than do the others; ...dead as he is in his own lifetime, he is the real survivor" (October 19, 1921). It was a matter of perspective, then. Having died to this life, one can *see* it more truly—especially in its animality.

Something in his bones. He tells Milena that the fear—characterized as the most terrible thing he has ever experienced or could experience, a monstrous flood that was his alone, yet inherent in all faith since time began—this gnawing fear is probably the best part of him, the part worthy of her love. "Even if I sometimes resemble a defense lawyer whom it has bribed" (August 9, 1920). Balancing his fear was his indifference.

"Human being" is described once in passing (in the second of three letters written to Milena on a very busy day [July 15, 1920]) as an "extremely vague and horribly responsible condition."

K. is "the only human being," writes one interpreter.[4] He is set off against the assistants, officials, lawyers, villagers, who, as types, are lodged in semblance (*im Schein einlogiert*). This means that the assistants, officials, and various others (above all, the vampish women in their hermetic-hetaeric intermediary roles) are typically more *vivid* as characters than K., who is the only human being precisely because he remains a characterless creature (if not exactly an underground man), a creature in essence dislodged, fitting into no secure niche and answering to

---
4 Walter Benjamin, in a letter of February 23, 1939, to T.W. Adorno.

no clear-cut vocation, other than that of "surveyor." The human being as fundamentally anonymous self: he responds as "we" would do. For the shadowy K. is in a position analogous to that of Kafka's readers, those engaged like him in essentially open-ended assessment as they take their way each time through the text. At once active and receptive in relation to the possible constitution of meaning, the reader is here obliged to be on the lookout for what may be clues beckoning from the dense, mazy undergrowth that threatens to obstruct all passage; there is information to digest at every turn, but one is constantly forced to consider what eventuates in terms of what lies hidden.

The action in Kafka's novels is generally organized not according to a logical sequence of events but topographically, according to an unfolding image space and cartography: each locale entered and surveyed discloses a particular story, deepening the overall mystery. The narrative delineates a progressive penetration—better, an ever-renewed sounding and feeling out—of some labyrinthine milieu, some infernal apparatus (an urban tenement, a remote snowbound village, a faintly disreputable hotel), naturally without any hint of arrival, of adequate coverage. Or, rather, such hints now and then seemingly do arise in unexpected corners of these unexceptional places, but they are immediately lost on the protagonist, who is either wholly engrossed in meditating the next stage in his strategy, so as to carry forward his appeals to an invisible authority and somehow justify himself, or else too wearied and distracted to get the message, if there is one. In the never-ending process of negotiating the ever-expanding corporate maze, all stations are preliminary, the paperwork never finished, yet there is a finality to the very bungling and imperviousness. It is a dream quest in which the goal is always right around the corner or through the next door, and in which the putative object recedes at every approach, fatally undecidable, as in some maniacal game of hide and seek. One awakens only to a new convolution in the dream.

The most jesuitical reasoning fills these works, so calm and circumspect in its endless meandering as effectively to conceal the fact that everything is hopelessly confused, as though mired in an element of shame and intrigue. Through this spiritual—as distinguished from psychological—morass, with its cloud of evil exhalations, the narrative necessarily proceeds by dint of meticulous and continually reoriented analysis, moving, like the doggedly inquisitive protagonist himself, from one provisional consideration, one temporary juncture, to the next, repeatedly shifting perspective as a new angle on the problem emerges, or sometimes a new construction of the problem as such, but in the end making no significant progress beyond charting a situation built largely on guesswork. As with the multiplication of voices and parodies in Joyce's revolutionary mimesis, the proliferation of discourse in Kafka's riddling, relentless parables entails a certain reduction in the value of what Balzac termed "drama." The action becomes more diffuse and metamorphic in obedience to the oceanic imperative of modernism. Everything, as in a dream, is simultaneously concrete and abstract.

Having "rigorously absorbed the negative element of

the age" in which he lived, Kafka saw himself as personifying an historical turning point—in this respect much like Schoenberg, his equal in sounding the colors of darkness: *Ich bin Ende oder Anfang* (I am an end or a beginning). He thereby makes a virtue of what he feels to be his own radical incommensurability, something reflected in the image of a burrowing nocturnal animal, a nameless ghost, or a shadow that cannot be drawn into the light. The corrosive "sense of nothingness" that often dominated his thought has for him a "noble and fruitful" side ("Letter to His Father"). Thus the uncanny cool serenity in his unprepossessing—more exactly, deadpan—presentation of the nightmare in his fiction.

Kafka inherits the realist tradition in prose fiction, the modern tradition—stretching from Cervantes to Flaubert and Chekhov—that broke with the epic world of heroes and monsters, but he returns with his realist methods and the language of report to the world of heroes and monsters. Of course, it is no longer the clearcut arena of action it once was; the monster and the hero are no longer so clearly differentiated. As with Joyce and Picasso, the epic world is distorted in the everyday, and traces of the forgotten village show up everywhere in the metropolis.

Josef K., at his carnivalesque arraignment, is the one who doesn't wear a badge.

The ending of *The Trial*: midway between the Book of Job and the pratfalls of vaudeville. From the perspective of a fundamental—and that means bottomless—nihilism, which in this regard can be compared to the perspective of a god, "the extremely ridiculous and the extremely serious are not far removed from each other."[5] This statement sheds light on the fabular dimension of Kafka's narratives, the peculiar rootedness of his radicalism. It was in such sublimated contradiction that Kafka himself lived and worked, being, for example, no less a man of the world and physiognomist of personal and professional relations than a self-lacerating and secretly exalted anchorite.

In step with his two stooge-executioners at the end, Josef K. is thankful—like Gregor Samsa, like Ivan Ilych—that it has been left him to say to himself what needed to be said (*mir selbst das Notwendige zu sagen*). Grace in falling.

Shame. There is still shame. That is Kafka's affirmation.

The dialectic of objectivity. By means of his late-night exploratory incisions into himself, Kafka overcame the world—in the process taking its side: "In the struggle between yourself and the world, second the world." This generous and severe self-decentering is no doubt the key to his disquieting and indeed demoniacal sanity.

He wrote to Felice Bauer, during the first year of their tortured engagement, that he was "made of literature," and that it was through his writing that he kept a hold on life. In his heart of hearts, as he said to frighten her, he doubted whether he was a human being.

In his walks around Prague, he tells Felice, he sought out places that were "as silent as the Garden of Eden after

---

5 Passing remark of an official in *The Castle* (from a passage deleted by the author).

the expulsion of man" (September 10, 1916). There, to disturb the peace, he would read Plato aloud to his sister Ottla, while she in turn gave him singing lessons.

"He does not live for the sake of his personal life; he does not think for the sake of his personal thoughts. It seems to him that he lives and thinks under the compulsion of a family, which, it is true, is itself superabundant in life and thought, but for which he constitutes, in obedience to some law unknown to him, a formal necessity. Because of this unknown family and this unknown law, he cannot be exempted" ("He" [1920]).

Cannot be exempted—from the personal.

When Kafka first started "fletcherizing" (endlessly chewing every morsel of his food) at the dinner table in his parents' apartment, his fuming, beleaguered father had to take refuge behind his newspaper until he got used to it. The family as breeding ground of the most delicate tyranny.

Kafka creates a hero who eats garbage.

Gregor's spirituality (the way to the unknown nourishment) emerges with his new animality—though there are hints of it earlier in the picture he cuts out and frames for his room. In both cases, beauty is connected to the erotic (the lady in furs, his sister's neck).

More explicitly than most other of Kafka's fictions, "The Metamorphosis" is concerned with cleanliness, with drawing boundaries and elimination, the unseemly connection between the sacred (the right food) and the obscene. As humorous. Humor was Kafka's salvation, a gift of writing as the most serious form of play. The marvelously detailed evocation of Samsa's bug body—leaving aside the fact that the bug himself is more humane than any of the humans—is a great achievement of the moral imagination, like Bloom's rat.

***

The Israelites, it has been said, were more history-conscious than any other people in the ancient world,[6] and it was precisely this uneasy presentiment of historical process, following on the conception of a fallen or disenchanted temporal nature, that was the signature of their modernity. Yet for Jesus of Nazareth, the last and most revolutionary of the Jewish prophets (one on whom, as Nietzsche observed, the archaic figure of the magic healer has been awkwardly superimposed by his followers), history hardly seems to exist: it is present only as the tradition—the scripture—that is radically renewed through him, the unaccommodated son of man, and thus no longer valid *as* tradition in the sense of precept. Having absorbed the lessons of the Law, the individual human being is now ripe for entry into Faith, that is, the present moment as living scripture, allegory in the flesh. This is nothing utopian or other-worldly. In its suddenly emergent and precipitous advent, the "now" eddying there in the "midst" of things takes precedence over all

---

6 Compare the classic account by Erich Auerbach, "Odysseus' Scar," in *Mimesis*, trans. Willard R. Trask (Princeton: Princeton University Press, 1953), pp. 3-23. What is at stake in this claim is not scientific historiography, which has various ancient precedents, but a stratified vertical dimension in experience and narrative, a distinctively Judeo-Christian interpretation of the retrospective-anticipatory momentum of time.

chronology—and therefore all eschatology. The task is henceforth readiness, understood as remembrance of the now: "Why do you not know how to interpret the present time?"[7] History becomes what it always effectively was in the ancient chronicles of the people: the bottomless well of teachings on which each secular generation draws, a continually reinscribed and fading palimpsest, witness to the ever-varied human cycle of incarnation, crucifixion, and resurrection through *time*. Which is nevertheless always at the beginning, vibrating in dream over the pregnant abyss.

The story of Adam and Eve is about the loss of the present in its living fullness—the expropriation of the Tree of Life and the cursing of the ground (*adamah*). The curse is never lifted, but the coming of a "new Adam" seeds the present moment with expectation for those who—like the people's prophets—watch and wait, stewards of the loss and of the promise. The image of the child in the gospel, the child one is called upon *to become*, is an image not of untouched innocence but of transfiguration in "knowledge," a reflective immediacy of experience possible only *after* the fall into self-consciousness, which in the primary instance is consciousness of nakedness—consciousness in shame, desire, estrangement, labor, and death. To be reborn as a child in this world is to unconceal nakedness. Overcoming a mode of thought in thrall to the world's antitheses, the messianic moment would eventuate in the midst of everyday sorrow (the age-old resurgent "waters" of which David sings), as a way to nearness eventuates through study and immersion in the

---

7 Luke 12:56. At issue is the opposition between *kairos* and *chronos*, or the transformation of *chronos* into *kairos*.

problematic.

Perpetual rupture of immediacy, the Fall propagates the curse of abstraction. But abstraction, as an intellectual-linguistic capacity intrinsic to and exceeding the capacity for naming, is from the beginning latent in humanity insofar as the Tree of Knowledge grows in Paradise. Abstraction has its blessings. For language is (perpetually) at the origin of things: God *speaks* the world manifold into being, calling forth from the primordial deep into every degree of celestial and terrestrial awakening. The book of the living is consequently pervaded by the chaotic dream energies of the deep, and the highest of God's creatures—man, the abstracted animal—is given to know the steepest descending.

The prodigal son is the true son—nothing could be more Jewish. The old humanism was already "above the law" in certain respects, as in the reversal of primogeniture that runs through the Book of Genesis. The supreme exemplar of faith for Paul is Abraham, the upstart stranger in a strange land, the pitiless wanderer burdened with visions and remembrances. Jewish conscience is from the first a burning, driven thing, skeptical above all toward itself in its obsession with purity, continually wrestling with an immanent yet impossibly distant divinity, and ready to venture everything for the sake of what was secretly promised in the wilderness to God's well-loved and much challenged problem child.

As spiritual go-between, Joseph descends into Egypt, black land, and is happily initiated into its mysteries. God makes him forget, as it is said, all his hardship and all his father's house—his provincial roots, in other words—and causes him to be fruitful in exile, like his haunted father Jacob before him, or like aboriginal Adam and Eve. But when the time of crisis he had earlier divined finally arrives for his family and all peoples ("all the earth"), he is suddenly confronted with what has been quietly forgotten and forgiven. He remembers his dreams. Having risen up out of the prison underworld he so readily made his own and become cosmopolitan overseer of the waking world, he now harvests the long reserved, momentous yield of the night, and through one more, not entirely solemn masquerade of "going down," one more hasty departure from the unsettled parental dwelling and one more test of patience in the extreme, he shepherds his father's scattered flocks—being no less (stage) manager than visionary, no less stern than tender-hearted. The "blessings of the deep" depend for their untoward gestation on the interpretation of dreams and what becomes of dreams.

On their way together up the mountain to which they have traveled at God's behest, Abraham and Isaac briefly converse: "Where is the lamb for the burnt offering?" "God will provide, my son." The answer is exemplary in its piety, but it is also clever and considerate, calculated to ease the lad's mind—for the time being—and to advance their incomprehensible journey. Furthermore, it is the truth. Abraham's cunning is sometimes indistinguishable from his love and from his bottomless trust in ("fear of") the hidden God, the invisible one who sees him. He is ready to alienate himself in the eyes of others and to fall on his face, if the Most High should give him the cue. On poor Isaac, however, is laid the additional burden of having to understand and forgive the singular apparition of his knife-wielding executioner father.

All animality leaves the nest and enters the encompassing world. All animality has this structure of opening and closure, expansion into the curvature of its own gravity. But only for humanity is this opening of a horizon something global. Humanity is the disruption of animal rhythm. To fall, in the biblical sense, is to be set apart.

But Eve sees that the fruit is good (to eat) before she has absorbed the knowledge of good and evil. Her delight in the sight of the fruit would seem to indicate that she is already distinctly human. Presumably she already knows, like any animal, that some fruits of the earth are good to eat and others not. It is evidently the food phenomenon that first teaches knowledge of good and evil, and it is interesting that knowledge here comes not in the form of bread but in the form of fruit.

Distance from the "ground"—from the earth as home, the naked body, the indwelling and overarching origin—is fundamental to the concept of sin: hence the importance of eyes in the story of Eden. At the same time, distance from the "world" is fundamental to the concept of redemption, which is in effect the harvest of sin. Eve's ardent gaze at the forbidden fruit in all its palpability and edibility mirrors God's happy perception that his work was good, although it is a distorted mirroring, as in a funhouse. At once ingathering (to the abyss of self) and dispersion (to the alien surround), the Fall is a parodic consummation of Creation, which is the force that divides things from one another and gathers each thing to its place. Both Creation and Fall, good and evil, exist by virtue of the articulating Word, the great cosmic tiding of individuation within a charged field of relations, the dialectic of being and nonbeing. In the biblical conception, language is more than human; or rather, it transcends the distinction between life and death, and is elemented of afterlives.

Continuous deliverance/ continuous fall: this is the structure of saying and being. The book of life. To seek to grasp what eludes us.

Two trees in God's pleasure garden, primal plantings in our nature, twin claims strangely intertwined though fatefully divergent: life and knowledge. What the story shows is that the world is latent in the garden and vice versa. It's like the relation between waking and dreaming, construction and absorption.

We are married to the world: one flesh. The trick is somehow to ward off mutual evisceration. It is a matter of interpreting signs, trafficking in ambiguities for the sake of truth. We can never be virgins again.

NOTES ON FILM

There is the old debate about the difference between silent film and sound film. The former goes through a rapid development, freeing itself from the framework of the theater, and reaches a brief but rich maturity before yielding its audience to the latter, which, with its return to theater via spoken dialogue, initially entails a regression in artistry. The unique formal language of silent film at its best—a language of gestures and of faces in constant permutation, hieratic and mask-like at times, given to passages of extreme acceleration and of near paralysis, with spatial layering as a rule and the sometimes scarcely perceptible proliferation of décor—this plastic language alternately austere and extravagant yields to the clever chatter and broad strokes of the talkies, and what has been called the institutional mode of representation. Such originally polyvalent devices as superimposition and lap dissolve are either eliminated or restricted to a relatively simple transitional function after the introduction of sound film, with its more exclusively linear imperatives. In silent film, these devices could suggest the interrelation of various time levels, the immanence of past or future in the present, or the interrelation of reality and fantasy, waking world and dream, presence and absence, and sometimes could do all this at once. No doubt sound film itself matured quickly enough in the course of the Thirties, repossessing the legacy of silent film (Vigo's *L'Atalante* and Ophuls' *La Signora di Tutti*, both released in 1934, attest to this), so that today one is inclined to speak of the evolving formal and thematic continuity of a single medium through different historical and stylistic periods rather than of two essentially distinct media with two essentially different ways of seeing. Nevertheless, to an eye sated with the technological sophistications of contemporary cinema, those shadowy and radiant images from the silent era often feel surprisingly new and strange, seem to resonate with the grandeur of a Giotto or the delicacy of a Simone Martini, or at any rate with the ritual aura of a Nadar or Mathew Brady, as if the ostensibly archaic mode in motion pictures suddenly revealed itself as the truly revolutionary one.

*

As the geometric forms in cubist painting threaten to overwhelm the human figure in their midst, the figure which nevertheless asserts itself in its humanity, so the visual design—the décor, the montage, the masquerade—threatens to overwhelm the characters in *L'Inhumaine*. But by the most delicate of (comic) maneuvers, the human element emerges intact and triumphs. The two central characters, who in their different ways are artists, together discover the higher humanism, which risks the *expérience* of danger and stands under the sign of death that is finally the sign of love.

Claire is poised between the Eastern despot and the Western scientist, between black magic and white magic, the jungle and the technological apparatus—just as the film as a whole mediates between a formalist and a mimetic imperative. By his elaborate machination, Einer appeals to the (inhuman) artist in Claire, the artist who had mockingly invited his suicide; he does so in order to overcome her (human) feelings of resentment at being tricked and in order to bring out her true humanity in mourning and love. His radio-tv transmission gives her what she wants (a world tour, if only virtual), while also providing for what *he* wants (which is to keep her there). Masquerade becomes the gateway to truth—the overcoming in exaltation of humanity.

The film makes explicit what is ultimately at issue in L'Herbier's earlier film, the celebrated *Eldorado*: the conflict between form and content, visual design and mimesis, *inhumaine* and *humaine*. It is a perfect pendant to *Eldorado*. Whereas the latter is a tragedy (mélodrame) of "mother love," *L'Inhumaine* is a comedy (féerie)—a comedy of seduction that turns into a comedy of death and resurrection. Each of the lovers, in this operatic *jeu*, has to die for the other to prove his or her humanity—for love is inhumane.

*

Cesare awakening in *Caligari*: at first to mere being and then, his eyes widening, to the enormity of it.

*

The ending of Epstein's *Fall of the House of Usher* should be compared to the ending of Murnau's *Faust*. The ideology of love: saved from/through the flames

*

Queen Kelly. A girl's entrance into sexuality. Her panties fall down, unbeknownst to her, opening the door to—

men. She gives her *heart* (her "panties") to the prince, in a delicious intoxication, a mist of white orchids, though there is a hint of playacting in it all. Stolen away from the nunnery (an innocent or a whore?), she enters the palace of true adoration, only to be driven out by the prince's intended, the queen, who is really a whip lady in a fur-trimmed black negligee. Another door is opening, now to a dark and savage place that, in its atmosphere of cozy corruption, is the exact opposite to the garden of princes. The palace gives way to the bordello, Europe yields to Africa. She comes of age. She refuses the fond prince (who in a vision—he was always a vision—asks her to "wait," to stay pure for him), and she gives her *hand* to the magnificently crippled old degenerate, with whom she manages the house of prostitution.—A true film fairytale.

Kelly's initial confrontation with the gun-toting, cigar-chomping old man on crutches, in the room of the dying madam, as he slowly approaches the bedside in his mechanical, relentless rhythm, leering at her through the gauzy bedcurtains that have replaced the orchids, is one of the great typifying moments of silent film.

The jealous queen who whips Kelly out of the palace and the dying madam who arranges Kelly's sacrifice to the old satyr: two aspects of the mother at whose bidding the girl loses her virginity. It is interesting that the old madam who presides over the horrible initiation rite, and then dies so that "Queen Kelly" can take her place, is seen as a figure of love, however stern. Like Kelly, she has tears in her eyes.

The projected conclusion is irrelevant to the film's significance. The film stands on its own as a consummate fragment.

*

The remarkable thing about *Pandora's Box* is that it establishes a standard for sober realism in film while exploiting the most melodramatic of material.

Pandora the nymph is pure image, pure surface; she resists all psychoanalysis and serves only to reflect the desires of those who surround her. She is the mystery at the heart of sober reality. All grow weak before her, make fools of themselves—even for a moment Death himself, in the person of Jack the Ripper.

*

The unforgettable moment at the beginning of *Earth*, when the dying worker asks for a pear. "He liked pears," it is said of him afterward. But it is a bit pat.

*

The New Babylon: more genuinely dramatic—but also more sober—than either *Potemkin* or *Earth* or *Mother*. The searing dramatic cell—whose theme is nothing less than the failure of the revolution—the story of the soldier and the midinette develops within a complex tissue of situations, as within a whirling, multifaceted bauble. The intercutting of the plot lines, the rapid editing (which, because it is integrated into a story, is never mechanical, like Vertov's), makes for extraordinary density—comparable only, in the universe of silent film, to the texture of such singularities as *A Page of Madness* or *Ménilmontant*. A plethora of contrasts and correspondences becomes apparent on repeated viewings. The explosive multiplicity ultimately subserves a dazzling coherence—but austerely dazzling. Its severity is grounded in the analysis of failure. The farmer who is caught in the middle, contemptuous of the bosses and drawn to the workers, cannot act on his feelings; he raises the shovel in a gesture of protest but, in his cowardice, miserably resigns himself to digging the graves of the Communards at the end. All that remains of their revolutionary zeal is a slogan, a white script traced on a stone wall—"Vive la Commune"—a historical record, an exhortation, a bitter irony, another ornament in the department store of the world: the ever-new Babylon.

The movement of the gravediggers in the background at the end, on the field of battle, reflects the movement of the dancers in the background at the beginning, in the Paris department store: a suggestive correspondence, both visually and thematically, by which background and foreground are "equalized," in Eisenstein's sense. The deadly intoxication of the Commune, its dance of death, pervades the film.

*

One can be a supreme master of montage and make a mindless film: *Napoleon*.

*

At the end of *Blonde Venus*, Ned tells Helen that home, with husband and child, is where she belongs. And she gratefully accepts his embrace. Yet the film has shown that the one thing that saves her from utter ruin is her talent and the spirit to put it to use. Where she *belongs* is on the stage. In the typical Expressionist schema that underlies all Sternberg's films, she must gradually descend into a hell of humiliation, must come face to face in a flop house with that old hag suicide—throwing all her hopes for happiness to the winds—before finally achieving redemption in the form of a career as artiste. But the ending does not acknowledge her achievement. The woman is entirely absorbed in the image of motherhood, before which the two decent men in her life quake helplessly, while the child is empowered. Or almost entirely: for she has a last song, a child's song, and her performance restores all that was lost, all their youth and innocence. (Though it doesn't restore the rich playboy, her good fairy and double, whom she must truly renounce, as he renounces her—all of this cogent only on a symbolic level, for on the literal level of the plot it is barely comprehended: Helen and Townsend both appear double in the mirror, and that is about the extent of the comprehension.) Only Dietrich's insouciance, the archness playing at the corners of her mouth, reminds us of the nihilism inhabiting her courage.—The ending, then, is confused and inane at the same time that it is tender and illuminating.

One of the keys to Sternberg's style—and it might be

said that he and Welles are the great stylists of American film—is the alternation of baroque articulation of spatial depth with plain, barely detailed surface: in *Blonde Venus*, the nooks and crannies of the bar into which cunning Helen leads the detective alternating with the fine pale mask of Dietrich's face.

*

Sunrise is a seductive movie. Why should those old vows of marriage move us so? And why should we in turn want to love and protect that paragon of virtue played by Janet Gaynor? No doubt the power of the acting is only one reason for this appeal. The resonance of the simple story—the sense of entry (through the twilight fields and over the fence) and initiation (across the waters) into an underworld, the sense of damnation and redemption—this rhythm of the parable, to which the acting, directing, writing, and cinematography contribute equally, is what really "moves us." It is only because we accept the violence of the hero, as reflected in virtually every milieu he passes through, that we embrace the ideals of purity and goodness embodied in his wife.

Master of the House is more sophisticated in its story and characterization; the women are neither vamps nor angels. Its comedy and drama are fully integrated into each other and there is no wasted detail. It is a more perfect film than *Sunrise*, but it perhaps does not cut as deep.

*

The dialectics of marriage in *Beauty and the Beast*: the woman initially the moral principle, man the animal. But for the marriage to work, the partners must change places, they must come to mirror each other; for it to get off the ground, it must enter the ground (the woods, the earth). In order to become a prince, the man must be filled with shame, and in order to fly from the bondage of serving her family, the woman must open out sexually, learning to love what she fears, becoming a goddess of the hunt.

Thus the importance of corridors. The house and the forest are ultimately merged.

The difference between the father's house and the beast's house is a difference in space, a difference that is palpable, that we feel. The space of the father's house is static, that of the beast's dynamic. The latter is a charmed space, in which everything is alive and in motion, a transformational space, a dream space. The former is the space of everyday. It is a matter of two rhythms, that of poetry and that of prose. In the course of the film, these image spaces, these rhythms are interwoven, as certain objects—the horse, the mirror, the glove, the key—communicate between them. Belle is transformed before the eyes of her family into the princess she always was, and the Beast behaves more and more like a bourgeois husband.

*

Dreyer's *Michael*: the slow, steady pacing, building a tide of inevitability, the attention to nuance of the most delicate sort, the opening out of time in the scenes, the subtlety and depth of the characterization—all this, as the film unfolds, is entirely unobtrusive, in keeping with the intimacy of the action, yet it comes together in the end to make an overwhelming impression. The characters move like tragic puppets through the layered décor—we see such puppets literally at one point in Michael's room—all of them driven by their passions and interlocked in their various betrayals and their bids for possession. Even the ancient steward of the household, a figure of undying, sublime devotion, is enlisted in Michael's schemes to appropriate the master's things. As a study of corruption and self-deception among the highly civilized, it has few peers in the world of cinema.[8]

Perhaps the subtlest irony in the film lies in the fact that Claude Zoret, "the master," is ultimately shown to be the truest *lover* of them all, the most long-suffering, generous, and forgiving (much more convincing as a hero of unrequited love—especially on his deathbed, with those seemingly bitter smiles—than is Gertrud in Dreyer's last film). His last words are an affirmation of true love, and they are taken up as the film's epigraph.

His *paintings*, on the other hand, are patently academic—"unreal" (*unwahr*), as a reviewer of one of his shows puts it. The callow insecure Michael, it is suggested, has

---

8 Its peers include *The Rules of the Game*, *The Earrings of Madame De*, *A Matter of Dignity*, *The Marquise of O*.

more real talent, though it emerges only in flashes, is undisciplined and unproductive, and may be a matter simply of greater vitality. At bottom, apollonian formal detachment is nothing without some degree of dionysian immersion in the subject matter, and this explains why Zoret's final achievement, an allegory of suffering solitude, may be supposed to have some truth to it after all. Dreyer's acid take on the art world goes together with his cool analysis of the artistic personality and his ruthless interrogation of destructive desire.

Vampyr is a fairy tale; there is no development of character. Nevertheless, there is a profound mimetic dimension, a profound humanity—mainly in the presentation of the family victimized by the vampire, in the father, the two daughters, the servants, above all the housekeeper (in the scene with the younger daughter when the father is shot). Unlike the protagonist, the young man who visits them, they resist the claim of the shadows that prey on them. The protagonist, artist-like, seeks out the shadows and, for a while at least, becomes a shadow himself. But the dream-journey into the land of the dead, into horror, has its heart in the mimesis of fear (in the father), of despair (in the older daughter), of infinite sorrow (in the housekeeper). The restless drive of the action—a drive to know (signaled by the book on vampires), to penetrate unknown corners—is immobilized at such moments of emotional depth, and we fall into a hell more real than any dreamt of in a fairy tale.

The hearth in the old peasant woman Marthe's house, at the beginning of *Day of Wrath*, is not seen again; it is nonetheless part of the intricate web of motifs in this film, for it shows up reflected in the "flame" in Anne's eyes and, of course, in the "stake." Love and death are merged in witchcraft. But it is through witchcraft that the other visual and verbal motifs are woven together: leaves, the window, the clock, the children. Woven in so subtle a way as to be almost imperceptible yet, as soon as one notices, shattering. The characters are fatally caught in this web of witchcraft, which is also a web of guilt. Once again, the living are in the hands of the dead: Marthe controls the action after she is burned at the stake. All the main characters are affected, except Absalon's mother, but it is she who denounces Anne and thus becomes the agent of Marthe (whose last words, practically, were "I'll denounce Anne"). *All* the women are witches—possessors of elemental power. In other words, the severe formal perfection of this film only heightens its drama.

Anne's sin is that she wants to be fulfilled as a woman. She is rejected by husband and lover. She has her dream—the scenes of idyll in nature, ironized by the fatal leaves everywhere—and her tears. At the end, with no one any longer to wipe them, she has her God.—Her confessing to witchcraft is either an admission of truth or else an expression of her guilt to her husband Absalon, an expression prompted by her despair at being abandoned by her lover. If the former, she is conscious of her mother's gift to her, the power to invoke (through "wishing"). And if she is not permitted to have a child—we remember her mother-in-law's passionate assertion that Absalon was the child she had longed for—she can at least revel in this power.

The repression of the woman, of the peasant, and their (secret) revenge: this too is a key element of "witchcraft." Which operates on several levels at the same time and is nothing if not ambiguous.—To her husband, Anne is childlike, "pure and clear," while to her lover she is mysterious and deep. She is both: innocent and demonic (like the childlike and vampirish Russian princess in *Michael*). This is demonstrated by the sequence in which she appears at the window to watch Marthe going up in flames.

Like *Day of Wrath*, *Ordet* is a movie of windows. Johannes, the Christ figure, is always crawling through windows, whether literally—the last time is to enact the departure and return of his sister-in-law Inger, so that she can herself return (from the dead)—or figuratively, as when he puts candles in the window to cast light into the darkness.

Through the window lies the world of those cows, horses, and pigs whose voices accompany the descent into death and the resurrection, the world of the "body": the dead body of the beloved is at the center of this film, Inger's body, to which her husband Mikkel clings in death and which he welcomes back to life. He too has crossed the threshold—into "faith"—and is no longer entirely of this world at the end. Through the window is heard also the voice of the wind, and at the end it enters from outside, with the visionary Johannes, to become the "breath of life." Which is the word of love, whose image no doubt is the child. The child is killed and cut to pieces, like Dionysus, and cast into a barnyard pail. His birth into death kills his mother. But these deaths are the occasion for the miracle, also imaged by the child, the dead boy's sister, whose smile is the sign of faith in the life rooted in death. Inger's "death" brings her neighbor Anne into the family, the child who has likewise just crossed the shadow line into womanhood. The two old men cease their bickering to witness the true word ("ordet") awakening. The doctor and the minister look on from a distance, the scientist more alert and receptive—he is the first to notice something strange about the corpse, shortly after Johannes enters transformed (though still not exactly of this world)—while the clergyman, whose love is salaried, remains uncomprehending and hostile, wanting only to put a stop to the proceedings. Mikkel has access to the window of faith; he can make the Kierkegaardian leap because his heart, as Inger says earlier, has always been full of love. He works with the animals on a daily basis, is resolutely "sane," and would never crawl through a window like a child.

All three of the men in *Gertrud* are sharply etched, devastating portraits. The poet: full of himself, a big baby, a self-acknowledged phrasemaker, but withal a man of the heart, who must weep and despair. The attorney: earnest and needy, whose dignity is belied by his frantic desire and concomitant self-deception, whose heartlessness is revealed in his encounters with those closest to him. And the young composer: a cad, arrogant in his genuine artistic gifts, but ignorant of the heart and of true civility (he cannot understand Gertrud's husband), unworthy of a woman's love.

As for Gertrud herself: she is not a character at all, not a self, hardly even a body, but rather, in her "ardent harshness," a mirror, a shadow in a mirror, there to tell the truth about the others, to reveal them in their sentimentality, frustration, and cynicism—the pure criterion by which the others are measured. She is, in short, the ideal woman who, in her positive and negative figurations, her light and darkness, dominates virtually all of Dreyer's surviving films, though nowhere so transparently as here.

The ideal woman—pure gesture. In fact, Gertrud is not taken seriously either as artist or as housewife: it's the man's production that matters in the world. She is not for this world anyway, as the final scene (the most mannered of all) makes clear: she is *always* seen as though shrouded for the grave. Whom has she loved really? It is an irrelevant question. Her love is absolute—beyond work, beyond the flesh. It is love in perfect renunciation. In other words, the most moth-eaten spiritualism posing as carnal love.

What saves this whole precarious conception, perhaps, is the suggestion of a monstrous narcissism in this angel of unhappiness. But can we salvage the Dreyer ambiguity in that line toward the end: "And in springtime I shall have anemones [over my grave]"? Hers is the most genteel of graves.

*

The chilling ending of *The Rules of the Game* is of a piece with the atmosphere of "farce and bitterness" (Sadoul) that prevails throughout. The film's sustained spontaneity, comparable in some respects to that of *L'Atalante* or *Under the Roofs of Paris*, though without a hint of lyricism, is fueled no doubt by the knowing improvisations. A principle of orchestrated diffusion rules nearly every scene, something as with the crowds in a Lumière. What Noël Burch calls "topographical reading" is required of the viewer. At issue here is Renoir's classic objectivity.

A sense of disaster hangs over the action, for all its gaiety. Hence, the power of diffusion in Renoir is finally worlds away from that of Tati, whose sunnier satire reflects an era of *post*-war reconstruction. (The scenes in the hallway with the guests going to bed remind one of Tati—and indeed of American slapstick. The rhythm of the film[9] recalls Capra and anticipates Sturges, though these directors lack the amplitude of Renoir.) The film coolly and lovingly delineates the physiognomy of collective madness but prescribes no corrective and offers no consolation.

1939: pervasive confusion that extends even to the hunt. All relations are based on self-deception. The German runs amuck without disrupting business as usual. The sacrifice of the "hero" is a mockery.—A courageous film in more senses than one.

---

9 Compare the beginning of *La Signora di Tutti*.

*

The Magnificent Ambersons is distinguished by a magisterial, darkly gleaming pictorial style, but the dialogue is excessively literary, even stilted. Presumably a baroque language was felt to be needed to match the baroque design of the visuals, and Agnes Moorehead and Anne Baxter show what was possible in this regard. But time and again the language seems merely flowery, as in a Victorian ladies-magazine story exemplifying true love's abnegation and the humbling of the proud heart. The dissolve from the shut front doors to the mother glimpsed through the curtained window, or the shot of the son's face reflected in the window pane through which he watches the retreat of his mother's lover (each man will lose his love), say more than all the "fine writing" in the world could do. What is most alive in this film, besides the tragedy of the three main women characters, are the spaces of that house.

The numerous low-angled shots in *Citizen Kane* have something puerile about them—very much the mark of a directorial debut. (Compare the more assured deployment of low angles in, say, *The Little Foxes*.) They are of a piece with the rather ridiculous distance separating Kane from his second wife Susan, as she sits doing a jigsaw puzzle on the floor, or with his broad condescension to her, as though she were a child (one that speaks secretly to the child in him), or with her emphatic vulgarity that so baldly sets off his brittle superbness. Altogether unsubtle. And this is true of the portrait of the two marriages in general. It does not approach the synopsis of marriage in Vidor's *The Crowd*.

*

The superimposition at the end of *Curse of the Cat People*, whereby the stranger becomes the friend and the friend the stranger. The ambiguity in the status of the apparition is maintained to the last: either the ghost providentially appears through the guise of the menacing young woman, or the child imagines she sees her friend in this sad rejected daughter. In either case, the child's trusting embrace softens the heart of the would-be murderess. She is saved by the ghost of a suicide, or else she suicidally embraces her own killer. What may seem like aesthetic flaws and gaucherie—the stiff ghoulishness of the parents and teacher, the voluptuousness of the secret playmate (noted by Agee in his 1944 review)—have a certain appropriateness. For it is not so much the canon of realism as the logic of dream or the logic of fairy tale (the child falling asleep in the woods) that holds sway here. Beneath the surface of decency and humaneness in this film lurks a rather darker cast of mind, the fruit of almost total estrangement, a child's despair. All of which goes to show that sometimes the most unassuming and even unconscious of movies may be the profound ones.

*

Gaslight is all about the Victorian domestic interior—about infinite degrees of light and shadow, manifold concealment, the most intricate disposition of space in a drawing room, about locked drawers, curtains, handbags, pockets, every sort of cover and recess. House as fortress, prison, ruin—the filmic equivalent of Dickens' Satis House. Full of ghosts.

Such a place is inevitably the scene of a crime, its traces everywhere obscured by the insidious fog, the equivocal gaslight. Circuitously, pausing at every untoward station, magnetized by the profusion of objects, we enter the madness of the Victorian interior.

In short, a cinematographic masterpiece, though the story is full of holes.

*

Eugene Loring's choreography in the "Marry Me" number in *Yolanda and the Thief* continually plays off a set of naturalistic moves—walking, staggering, struggling to escape, and other comic business. Often the transition from naturalism to dance is impossible to pinpoint. Loring himself appears with the group of ladies, gents, and jockeys dressed for the races; he plays a sort of puppet master, and his moves are a synthesis of naturalism and dance, so smooth and underplayed as hardly to seem a dance at all, wonderfully arch in its reflection of the motif of "pulling the strings," manipulating the victim (and getting paid for it). The movements in and out of dance—if the notion "out of dance" be allowed here—are even subtler in "Limehouse Blues" (*Ziegfeld Follies*); the choreographic accentuation of the music is extraordinarily varied, mimetic, and everywhere precise (even when off the beat). In the scenes on the street, where Loring appears as the Costermonger, it is as if the actions remain naturalistic and *at the same time* articulate the music. At other points, as when Astaire trails Bremer on the street, he dancing and she walking and window shopping, there is a distinct counterpoint of the danced and the natural movement, or of dream and waking life. The concluding scene, in the shop, begins entirely naturalistically, but with the dropping of the fan (key motif) there is a sudden, almost imperceptible shift into dance: the movements of the actors, of their shadows, of the camera, even of the smoke in the air, all work together in rhythm with the song—or rather songs, for the musical texture itself is complicated by melodic superimpositions and dissolves, injecting a fine dissonance into this simple tale of old Chinatown.

*

In that post-war Hollywood parable, *It's a Wonderful Life*, the dream sequence, the "spell," portends a rude awakening from the dream (of small town life)—suggesting that no binding relation is real except the relation to the angel, and even he is gone the moment you call on him; that community is born only to be sabotaged and the good man (at the window of Potter's office, at the end, yelling "Merry Christmas" with his arms outspread) crucified; and that in this potter's field, before the wall of snow, everyone is a stranger—and having accepted all this, his full powers of hearing restored for one moment of his adulthood, George Bailey returns to ordinary life as a child for whom *money* is entirely unreal: that is the true bail.—At heart a desperate film, intent on or trapped into concealing its despair about America, indeed sugar-coating it.

*

It is the protean quality of the mother, in addition to her keen eye, her craftiness, and her unflagging sense of justice (beyond mere "rules"), that the remembering young artist before the mirror, in *I Remember Mama*, soberly and lovingly makes her own, as she becomes a progenitor of a different sort.

*

The best thing about *The Quiet One* is Helen Levitt's documentary photography, especially the scenes of street life so reminiscent of her gritty wondrous still photographs. Agee's spare and keen commentary is peculiarly detached from the action, though the final words of hope in view of the infinite corridors of despair that make up Harlem are fully attuned to the visual music. The story of the boy, presented as a "case study" with a studied avoidance of sentimentality and easy solutions, is, for all the naturalness of the performances (intercut with documentary footage), a bit contrived in its very typicality, and strikes one as dated in comparison to the fleeting revelations of some of those street scenes.

*

In its galvanic rhythmic tautness, its almost atonal yet systematic sounding of intimate vulnerabilities and unexpected perils within a labyrinthine urban milieu, and in the salutary moral skepticism that speaks from its unflinching regard for the "mixed motives" of human action, *The Asphalt Jungle* sets a standard for film noir.

*

Night and the City: the eternal con man on the run, with momentary precipitous asylums, deep into the byways and backrooms of the nocturnal city—the city that finally and irrevocably encloses him in its noose, before one last lurch for redemption. Utterly of the moment and blind to consequence, his last scheme fails like all the others, and he is quite literally strangled and left to sink in turbid waters. But, unlike the others, this scheme is noble in the classic or antique sense the film wants to evoke (by its setting in the world of "Greco-Roman" wrestling). With finally no way through the intricate meshes he has himself diabolically fashioned, the hapless protagonist determines on sacrifice to gain the bounty for his beloved and, in a glorious frantic sequence at the film's end, runs headlong, as though victorious, to his death.

*

In the last scene of the '38 *Camille*, Garbo's slightest movement, gesture, flicker of expression in body, face, voice carries a world of meaning. One must go to another star of the silent film, Gloria Swanson in *Sunset Boulevard*, to find a comparable—that is, equally bold and incomparable—melding of naturalism and symbolism.

Sunset Boulevard is so fully realized that it's hard to say what it's about. On the one hand, it is an ironic modernist transfiguration of screwball comedy, and, on the other hand, it is a consciously "archaic," operatic descent into

Sternbergian décor, the Sternberg grotesque. (Dreier and Seitz are the overt links to Sternberg.) The eternal feminine, woman as principle of chaotic-redemptive vitality, puts on the tragicomic death mask and, mesmerized by a dream past turned nightmare, dances undaunted—sovereign and pathetic—into "the dark" of the camera eye.

*

"Miss du Bois?" Magic words. As she lies there on the floor of Stanley Kowalski's tenement apartment, held down by a female attendant of the insane asylum to which she's headed, humiliated, shattered, and reduced, she looks up into the monstrously ugly, deathlike countenance and smiles sweetly. His courteous address, his gallant arm, and she is his, is herself again, just passing through in all her disruptive, ridiculous, and faintly tragic singularity, before the commonplace reasserts itself. Blanche du Bois lives in a dream world compounded of fantasy and memory, but she knows what's what. On the other hand, gentle Stella cannot recognize the monstrous, refuses to believe her husband capable of it, and so puts her crazy sad sister away—after Stanley has brutally and systematically destroyed the invader.

At the end of *Baby Doll*, the child wife walks through the littered yard of the derelict mansion Archie Lee has bought her, with his whiskey bottles hidden in the few remaining pieces of her furniture, with gaping holes in the walls through which he spies on her, and animals everywhere, and with Archie Lee himself handcuffed and about to be carted off by the sleazy town marshal for going berserk at the sight of her carrying on with the "foreigner," the wily "wop" Vaccaro, new man in the Old South, a man who gets what he wants, and more, and who in revenge for willful arson, as he keeps pointing out, has possessed himself of everything Archie Lee has left, including his wife and his cook, Aunt Rose Comfort. "Today's my Baby Doll's birthday," Archie Lee says in a subdued voice edged with bitterness, as she slowly walks past, ignoring him, her musing face partially lit in the shifting chiaroscuro. Midnight bells have just sounded the end of a long fall day, the day before her twentieth birthday—harsh and intermittently stormy, peppered with falling leaves everywhere. Amid the general wreckage of her marriage and household, she has come of age. In the brief final sequence, she affirms her solidarity with her pathetic, half-senile, but dignified old aunt in the face of all those unscrupulous men. This festive nihilistic comedy (condemned by the Legion of Decency on its release) ultimately sides with the victims.

The shots of frail Aunt Rose in the empty front hall toward the film's end, with the front door wide open to the night, and the tattered leaves blowing across the threshold, lend an unearthly quality to the acutely class-conscious social realism. There is of course a precedent for this in the literature of the American South.

*

Mizoguchi is a great master of the movie ending. And nowhere is this more evident than in *Yokihi* (Princess

Yang Kwei-Fei), where, after the magical transition to the final sequence shot—actually a burn out to whiteness, from which the final shot burns in, registering the passage of many years—the tears turn into ghostly laughter. The incantatory dialogue of the two souls counterpoints the subtle movement of the camera through the dying emperor's room, past the still statue of the beloved, the hangings, the furniture, the gleaming objects all still as death, toward the passage at the other end of the room, where suddenly things are in motion: the curtains are billowing, leaves are falling and scuttling across the floor, and we are drawn with this wind, with the rising waves of laughter, into the luminous threshold as the film ends. The final shot is a good example of Deleuze's point about Mizoguchi's lateral movement, "which creates the space instead of presupposing it."

*

As Ricci pursues the old man through the mission, in the middle of *The Bicycle Thief*, he and little Bruno pass by the central aisle with the two priests in pursuit of *them*. The two brothers pause to kneel before the altar, Bruno pauses likewise and kneels, but Ricci tears by heedless. What are we to make of this? It is part of a pattern, of course, the pattern of Ricci's neglect—neglect of his wife carrying the buckets at the beginning, of his son throughout the day, and now of Jesus and all he stands for. Antonio Ricci is so desperate to earn a living that he forgets—or nearly forgets—about living. (In his apartment with his wife, in the restaurant for a moment with Bruno, and finally at the end in his shame and grief, he comes alive as a man.) The visit to the fortuneteller brings back the image of the cross and the idea of the moment—"subito," now or not at all—the idea of readiness. What the fortuneteller says is confirmed shortly afterward on the street: the thief appears *now*. Is it Ricci's failure to live in this "now"—a failure for which capitalist society, presumably, is ultimately responsible—that is signaled by his forgetting to kneel in the mission church? Is Bruno the child therefore to be considered closer to Jesus, to faith ("Fides" is the brand name of the stolen bike), to forgiveness? It is the presence of the child that saves his father (from prison). To be sure, the film never shows its cards, never discourses outright. We laugh at Bruno's hasty kneeling, and the mission establishment is shown to be at least as worldly as the well organized charlatan who dispenses "spiritual" advice. Ricci's not bothering to kneel is a comment on the church's irrelevance. Neither social reform nor philanthropy is the answer, we surmise. There is no justice and there is no remedy in the world of this film. There is hope perhaps—but only in the full experience of desolation. It is something no less sociological than theological. Which points to the largely unnoticed mystical strain in this neorealist classic.

The image of the child—of children—dominates the ending of *Umberto D* as well, where there is another redemption in despair, another opening of the "now" beyond the crushing burdens of the city, with its implacable facades and internal disintegration. But the image of the child is not integrated into the main action of *Umberto D*, as it is in the earlier film; and the sober and rigorous sociology that frames that action is missing from the ending—which is *merely* theological. The scene in the park at the end is wholly absorbed into metaphor. Or nearly so: the wave of children expresses the joy of the old man in playing with the little dog whose trust (*fides*) he has regained—the joy released, by a dialectical reversal, from the experience of near suicide. The revelation, in other words, is grounded psychologically, in the character's emotions, and the metaphorical is grounded in the documentary.

The danger with DeSica and Zavattini—and it is a danger incurred by a host of modern filmmakers following in their steps—is that despair will become abstract, become merely a gesture, an ideology. Witness *Miracle in Milan*.

*

In his notes on "cinematography" (as opposed to "cinema," i.e., photographed theater), Bresson has provided hints for an appreciation of his highly original concept of action in *Diary of a Country Priest*. He speaks of a kind of drama that depends on the "march" of non-dramatic elements, which is to say, the "visible parlance" of faces, bodies, objects, houses, roads, trees, fields—these elements drawn together in a rigorous dynamic of "currents and cross-currents," as in a Cézanne. Such drama involves the generation of emotion by means of the resistance to emotion—a resistance allied to the powers of silence, stillness, blankness. He speaks of inner movements that are seen (the formula is worthy of Dreyer), and of something necessarily ineffable in the images, something that again resists expression. It is "necessity," not beauty, he strives for, the necessity residing in the "automatism" of ordinary life, in those unconscious or half-conscious gestures and actions that reveal far more than do deliberate actions. Accordingly, the scenes in this drama will be oriented not toward information, let alone grand discovery, but toward "divination." Each passage in the action should intimate some withheld revelation. To be sure, the "wonderful little priest" makes his discoveries. He works his way into the dark corners of his parish, all of them full of malice, and learns the lessons of futility. But he also learns, courtesy of his own agonizing death, that all is grace. It is a matter of the proper perspective, or rather the gift of detachment from "the proper," from the world of the living—for in "God's world" the living and the dead are as one.

Thus his joy and his mourning are inseparable: this is what he communicates to the countess who, in a central scene, is suddenly able to accept the loss of her long-dead child. The priest himself gains perspective in writing his diary, an activity to which we are privy in the remarkable sequences that form the backbone of the film—sequences of inscription in audio-visual relay (the words being written on the page that appears on the screen are simultaneously spoken by the priest in voice-over). These spectral images of writing trace the ineffable meaning of the drama, of the passion, at issue in this film text. The film is the diary writ large, its action a living scripture.

There is something unconvincing about the ending of *Mouchette*—something arbitrary. Why could she not have been the sort to bear it out? She is a brave and devoted young woman; all the little protests she sounds against the degrading environment she lives in testify to resilience. So why wrap herself in her mother's shroud and roll into the water?

"Mouchette ... is found everywhere," explains the director, "in wars, concentration camps, torture chambers ...." No less than Godard (who, in other respects, seems his cinematic antithesis), Bresson has a message to send. Of course, the ending is carefully prepared by everything that comes before it—the tightening snare of the milieu (not unlike the lowlife milieus in *Coeur fidèle*), the systematic exclusion effected by the people and institutions of her community, the murderousness in the air. With the death of the mother, it is made clear, all hope and care are gone. But it is precisely in this formal closure, by which the ending is supposed to feel predetermined *rather than* arbitrary, that the film's tendentiousness emerges. Teenagers choose suicide often enough, and sometimes on grounds far less cogent than those presented here, but the ending unthinkingly turns its back on probability as a principle of character and action in order to make a facile political statement. What Bresson likes to call "the life of the film" is thereby compromised.—Compared to Satyajit Ray's *The Postmaster*, *Mouchette* seems hysterical.

L'Argent too: the action is hypnotic in its power of immediacy, but the logic of the plot obeys a simplistic equation of despair. Having been unjustly branded a criminal, Yvon becomes one for real: the victim, once again, of a bad world. Having lost his job, child, and wife, he steals money and kills a family. And then gives himself up to the society that first taught him to transgress—for there is no escape any more. Everything follows with iron necessity from his eventual conviction and imprisonment for being accomplice to a robbery; but, given his love for wife and child, given his pride, why should he have agreed to participate in the first place? The question is not seriously entertained in the film (as it is in Dostoevsky, Zola, or Dreiser). There is no time for questions in the rush to indict the institutional world. The blankness of the protagonist in this case signals the abdication of thinking. A certain lobotomized sensationalism prevails.

*

Kurosawa is the most high-minded of directors. His thematic tendency (the restoration of faith in humanity, the indictment of poverty, etc.) is related to this. Although more refined in sensibility and far less theatrical, he nevertheless recalls the didactic Abel Gance in some respects. Even more, he recalls the didactic John Ford.

The night-on-the-town sequences in *Ikiru* are memorable for their brilliantly textured mise en scène—Kurosawa is practically unrivaled in his treatment of that fundamental cinematic subject, the life of the streets—but the film's ending is weak literarily. The image of the dying man on the swing swinging is too pat, too far removed from the horror of death evoked in the waiting room of the doctor's office at the beginning. The comparison with *Ivan Ilych* implicit throughout the film completely breaks down at this point.

Mifune's performance in *The Idiot* ranges over an unprecedented emotional gamut; it is a beautifully controlled descent into madness. Had such authentically old-world *nobilitas* been seen on the screen since Seastrom's outlaw? And where else in such intimate communication with the whooping and hopping demonic? Ultimately, with the catatonic.

*

Satyajit Ray absorbed the lessons of De Sica and Renoir—lessons about structuring a narrative according to patterns of daily life—and the example of their rich and harsh humanity, but he was in some ways a greater poet than either De Sica or Renoir. That is, he was more of a thinker, and his imagery, camera movement, have a metaphysical resonance, in addition to a beautiful rhythm, lucidity, and honesty. This is already fully apparent in *Pather Panchali*, as, for example, in the scene at the end when little Apu destroys the evidence of his dead sister's crime by throwing the stolen beads into the pond: the ruckus itself is long forgotten among his relations and neighbors, and it is only he, Apu, who will remember it. The image of the weedy water's swallowing up the coveted ornament becomes the seal of his memorializing of his sister Durga, that reckless and tender force of life. For the agitated surface of the present does not entirely close over the object from the past; through the weeds, as we see at the end of the shot, is an eye-like opening into the depths.

The figure of the old aunt in *Pather Panchali*, often viewed at a low angle, in shadow or in firelight, has an almost Shakespearean grandeur and cackling poignancy.

*

Le beau Serge is quite consciously a primitive—in its look and feel, in that "rough" quality so different from Hollywood gloss, in its attunement to the routines of village life, and in its simple-minded psychology. The plot is really quite corny—for all the local color and vivid reality of the mise en scène. The seasonal rhythm of the story—its gradual descent into winter (sacrifice and new birth)—is epitomized in the prolonged transition shot at the doorway to the hero's room, where, as he resolves to stay and save the soul of the dissipated friend who's just beaten him up, we see, in lyrical superimposition, the snowflakes beginning to fall as he leans his head against the door.

He is at the threshold, the moment of decision that shows what he is (a *true* Christian, unlike the priest), and the obliterating cold awaits him. Such a moment is haunted by the future it is about to bear.

The inversions in *Les Cousins* are both formal and diegetic. The visitor is now the provincial, but in both films he is the saint (spurned by his girl) and the native is the sinner. The cinematography is appropriately more dynamic and asymmetrical here to reflect the Parisian setting and sophistication. But the story line is just as corny.

*

The ending of *L'Avventura* creatively cites the ending of *The Bicycle Thief*: the forgiving consoling hand. And throughout, in his whole approach to storytelling, Antonioni takes up De Sica's methods. Place exerts its mesmerizing effect on the characters and the action, which unfolds at its own pace, but always subject to the gravitational pull of an absence (a stolen bicycle, a missing girl), taking the form of a (futile) search that turns inward. For at the end, after all the divagations and the fleeting respites (lunch in the restaurant, clowning in the hotel room), the two pairs are reunited in their guilt and anguish. The woman and the child are *witness* to the man's transgression and remorse.

Of course, the chief witness is Anna herself, especially after she has vanished from the party. Her gaze on the lovers is felt everywhere—from housefronts, passing trains, windows and walls in hotel rooms, deserted squares—usually at a distance. But sometimes she is right there in bed with them, freezing their love with the question "Why?" that they bandy back and forth—her question, inescapable. It is as if, after she disappears from the action, her gaze becomes one with that of the camera.

*

A Taste of Honey is a keen and immensely gentle film, full of somber festivity. It looks the blankness right in the face, without getting particularly riled or losing its sense of the continuity of life. With the return of the mother, the prosaic realism, never far removed from the spirit of humor, assumes a mythic magnificence—and without any corn about "growing up." Shelagh Delaney's apolitical script is perfectly harmonized with Richardson's and Lassally's politically drenched visualization. Perhaps the only real weakness is in the recurrent motif of children singing and playing, which seems forced, or precious, but which is also, as an expression of playfulness and renewal, a characteristic detail and the signature of an epoch (the Sixties), even though derived from *Umberto D.*

*

A chronicle of the counterculture and its gesture of rebellion. In *Saturday Night and Sunday Morning*, the alienated (anti-)hero grudgingly conforms, having sown his wild oats. In *The Loneliness of the Long-Distance Runner*, he protests against police mentality, victorious in defeat. In *Billy Liar*, he impotently seeks to reconcile bourgeois reality with his dreams. And in *Morgan!* he gives up on society and, driven crazy, drops out, not without leaving offspring.

*

Lolita is a study in hipness. Those Ohioans, those Americans (they're *all* middle Americans) are so unhip, so vulgar and inelegant. The dramatic interest of the film is in the slow but inevitable degradation of the paragon of elegance—Mason's "sincerity" makes it all the more exquisite—as he "falls in love." He then outdoes the Americans in vulgarity: the vulgarity of jealousy and possessiveness, the vulgarity of schemes of deception, the vulgarity of murder and revenge. And at every step of the way, he is goaded by the relentless devil of hipness in the persons of Quilty and Darkbloom, who are all style, all labyrinthine mask. Their little dance at the beginning, her very look, are a parodic—that is, hip—evocation of the hip (as a cultural type).

The musical score sets the machinations of destructive passion into the framework of kitsch, while the names of the characters and places work to demean the action. It's like a constant put-down. Over and above the wonderfully detailed performances, the film is always winking at the audience: "Are you hip?"

*

When Guido comes to the mirror, toward the beginning of 8½, we see a haggard-looking man—seedy, flybitten, almost doltish in his satanic brooding—who struggles to wake up from his dreams but can only relive them, waking *to* the nightmare. It is a riveting portrait of the artist before the merciless-merciful mirror of art. But after the opening scene, this abject quality is suppressed, and in its place comes long-suffering ironic nobility, the director as hero. To be sure, there is still a clownish aspect to this super-elegant man, but it is the tragic clown, a little like Alceste, who also feels put upon, finds everyone a bore, runs from them, but needs them more than he likes to admit. And after all, what's so special about being unable to love? Of course, the film really considers its hero's love, in its tender and wry acceptance of practically everything, to be as far above that of the colorful crowd as, say, Citizen Kane's love is above that of his second wife.

All too Wagnerian, in either case.

The figure of the chattering critic—the whole hackneyed thematic concern with "belief," "meaninglessness," "authenticity"—merely betrays the film's own academicism in the midst of all that unforgettable vitality. It is very earnestly "existentialist." The coy aesthetic self-reflexiveness follows from this.

A little like *Wild Strawberries*, the film is organized in terms of the people in Guido's life, his encounters with them—in the main, his failures and betrayals. All the hallucinatory memory- and dream-interpolations have at their center some beloved person or persons. These encounters form a constellation, which is the inconspicuous structure of the film. The sad festive ending renders this as a dance of death, lays out the string of relations like a cherished necklace on a moving display, each jewel a priceless souvenir of his love and remorse, each for a moment highlighted in the memory-laden perception of the artist, who has finally conquered and redeemed the unhealed hopeless world, the hopelessness in himself, by reflecting it in his magic mirror, simultaneously remaining true to the dreaming child within him, the wondering spectator and star attraction at a circus.

Whereas Cabiria's tearful joy, at the end of Fellini's earlier film, springs from her indomitable character and her feeling of gratitude to be alive, so that the smallest sign of friendliness seems a miracle, Guido's transcendence of despair is philosophical-aesthetic: he solves the problem of how to make the film by embracing the chaos rather than trying to escape it. He makes the film of his life, the film we are seeing, document and artwork in one. The movie set is finally presented as such, as bare apparatus, at once "messy reality" and "pure symbol."

Cabiria is set apart, in the language of the Pauline epistle. That's what is established by the keyhole shot, suggestive of the primitive iris, in the scene at the actor's villa. Her deep emotion at the sight of the lovers embracing is simultaneously that of the viewer-voyeur (at a silent film) and that of the sacrificial victim, the loser. She is both moved by their fulfillment and full of pity for her own forlornness. Sad clown, God's fool.

In *8½*, during the magical magician sequence at the spa, the shadows moving on the wall of the children's bedroom, in Guido's sudden remembrance, recall the mechanically dancing shadows in *Vampyr*. The images of memory, the fruitful dead, art's necessary commerce with the underworld.

*

At the end of *Cold Comfort Farm*, this relatively unheralded gem of film humor, there is an elegiac note for the passing of all that appalling barbarity—victim of the "tidying up," the organizational skills of our winsome heroine. Renewal is here predicated on a certain hygienic destruction, a final dissolution of the aristocratic family gone to seed. The modern woman in all her conveyances (motor car, railway, aeroplane) is set against the fierce archaic mother grieving before the shrine of her wandering younger son. Being modern ourselves, we laugh at the mother's lamentations—or, more precisely, at the candle-lit shrine to lover-boy—but, despite the squawking mocking geese in the background, her sorrowfulness and wide-eyed terror are not entirely wiped out in her burgeoning reformation, wherein divination yields to psychoanalysis and she becomes a perfect case study. The smashing success of Flora's enlightenment project (which, however, cannot penetrate the mystery of ancestral guilt linking her father, Robert Poste, to the Starkadder clan) is accompanied by the most ineffable melancholy.

The old Adam is the only member of the household who does not change, any more than twigs or cows do, but he does enter the modern world, moving his slightly stubborn but beloved herd from the gloomy Elizabethan cottage, with its twisted and morbid obsessions, to the natty Restoration-style mansion.

Compare *Cold Comfort Farm* to another cinematic *jeu* by a master at the end of his career: *Same Old Song*—the one very English as the other is very French, but both making sophisticated use of popular traditions as, with an unerring instinct and a light touch, they weave together multiple plot lines (representing the variegated strata of an evolving social milieu) like a technological Prospero. Is not such accomplished intellectual playfulness rather rare in the cinema?

In *A Kind of Loving*, which shows the director's roots in documentary and urban neorealism, the comedy of the ending is so brilliantly muted as to be really appreciable only in recollection. After a long chilly night on the bench at the depot, the protagonist encounters in quick succession the cold shoulder of sister and mother, only to be finally enlightened by his father in the greenhouse, symbol of spring, as to his own ridiculous position: you'll be the clown if she won't take you back! The heroes of Schlesinger's later films, from Billy Liar through Joe Buck to Madame Souzatska, are repeatedly being made to look like fools while remaining in their different ways uniquely heroic.

The comedy usually has a satirical edge and not infrequently verges on the grotesque. It might be said that Schlesinger's great subject, like Stroheim's and Pabst's, is decadence. The purest example is no doubt *The Day of the Locust*, that ultra-refined foray into grossness of all kinds. The complex humanity in evidence in his earlier and later films is here systematically debarred and reduced, and each scene is carefully designed to expose some major or minor outrage. Story, character, and theme—the moral, psychological, and political inquiries into corruption, repression, mass hysteria—all recede before the orchestration of dissolution, the masquerade of apocalypse.

The extreme low-angle shot from under the furniture, in *The Believers*, shows the father, in his consternation at the superstitious maid who thought to protect his son, leaving the boy's room with the worthless (as he thinks) and sinister-looking fetishes in hand—all except for the one under the dresser that comes into view with its lighted candle in the foreground, as he crosses toward the door behind, and establishes through its uncanny point of view a particular presence in the room, a presence ensconced, or even embodied, in the sundry material objects, and in this case a demonic presence, with its innocent eye.

*

Great film-making does not necessarily result in a great film: witness David Lynch's *Lost Highway*. His carefully distilled rhapsodic savagery—he is the Lautréamont of American film—leaves no space or time for thought. With its absence of "character" in the conventional sense (the "story" is linked mainly by the motif of doubles and of observation), the film has the depth and meaninglessness, the arbitrariness and inevitability, of a dream.

One thinks of the aestheticism of French films of the Twenties: the visual deformations in *Eldorado*, the layers of road unrolling in *L'Inhumaine*, the paralyzed durations in *La Chute de la maison Usher*. But also of the German aesthetic of humiliation and degradation.

Lynch's mastery of montage—as more or less distinguished from mimesis—extends to the vertical: the counterpoint of sight and sound. He is not just the most authentically "painterly" of contemporary American directors but also the most "musical." Which is to say, the most purely "cinematic."

The Elephant Man makes us wait before showing us the monster, thus participating—quite knowingly—in the exhibitionism that eventually kills him. He participates in it himself: the violent orgy in his room is immediately preceded, and as though brought on, by the monster's display of vanity, his reveling in his new toilet articles in a crooked little dance of joy. At heart, he's a dandy.—Of course, he's also a saint, suspended between heaven and hell, soul and body, delicacy and brutality. Such beauty in grotesquerie is an expression of the film's medievalism, its gothicism (complete with devils and hellfire). The element of camp, which Lynch so readily indulges elsewhere, and which could easily have overwhelmed this film, is kept down throughout; the many tears are never mocked at. Only in the theater scene at the end, the heavenly representation of hell (the "dungeon") on earth, is the campiness in evidence on the stage—necessarily so. Like any child, the monster is delighted by the procession of monsters. After his triumph in the theater, and with his mother's voice—which is the voice of the clouds and wind and stars—in his ear, he can finally lay himself down to sleep, his maidenly soul unstained by all the violations.

*

Like David Lynch, but in a wholly different and equally original, equally cinematic idiom, Guy Maddin flirts with camp in his films. He resists and overcomes the temptation not exactly through primal dramatic interest, as with Lynch, but through literary sophistication, meaning not just highly literate scenarios, their language often precariously balanced between the baroque and the most up-to-date, but an intricately informed—both mesmerizing and satirical—creative appropriation of the history of cinema, of its vast stock of narrative and audio-visual devices, gestural devices: an appropriation reminiscent at times of Joseph Cornell and the Surrealists, but more concerned with telling stories or, rather, playing with them. It is likely this bold and constantly experimenting practice of critical reinvention of the past—epitomized in the humorous and vertiginous historiographic interventions of *My Winnipeg*—that is largely responsible for the great stylistic distinction of his work.

*

Through his meticulously worked-out improvisation techniques with his highly resourceful repertory company, Mike Leigh has perfected a kind of vernacular tragicomedy or, better, bourgeois trauerspiel (mourning play)—something already in evidence in the harsh and gritty lyricism of the punk-era television movie *Meantime*, with its anarchic subversion of philanthropy, and at an apex in *Another Year*, which is possibly the best movie of its social-realist type since *Sunday, Bloody Sunday*. It is a wry and penetrating critical meditation on new-millennium therapy culture (the casting is crucial here), unfolding in full cognizance of the opposite, much more deleterious, boneheaded tendency of culture. And in full cognizance of our common mortality. It is about incurable unhappiness, a talent for unhappiness. The film follows a professional therapist around, the principled "Martha" character, and seems by its respect for the details of behavior to be centered in her sane, calm perspective, as in that of her archly generous bearded husband, these two hard-working responsible citizens. But at the end, in a moment reminiscent of the scene in the car in *Wild Strawberries*, when the voices of the young people fade out and there is just the radiant face of the weary old man being sung to in the front seat, it focuses decisively, after tracking slowly around the dinner table while the complacent chatter about travel in the Greek islands is slowly muted, on the unkempt "Mary" character, in all her nervous self-absorption and wild sadness.

*

We do not so much see as feel the background, Dreyer says—a marvelous and very important formulation. For it indicates that film is not just what is called a visual medium.

And it is not simply that the element of story involves our emotions, memories, and imagination, so that our perception is at every moment embedded in a shifting context of psycho-physiological impressions. It is also that our perception of space itself—or spacetime (for in film, more conspicuously than elsewhere, space is always in motion)—is an embodied perception, is part of the body of space perceived. Articulated by light and shadow, by varying shapes and hues, the depths of space and its surfaces resonate; the world of things is alive. Film reality, as Jean Epstein puts it, is animistic.

Another critical point made by Dreyer: atmosphere conditions the perception of action. Insofar as place is evoked, there will be some degree of atmosphere. Again, atmosphere and place, in film, are themselves dynamic—more precisely, rhythmic—expressions of a fundamental spatiotemporal action and structuration, a bodily configured spacetime. For the perception of space in time is sensuous, physiological, without being confined to any particular sense. This means that, in an "atmospheric" film, the imagery bears a considerable subliminal weight or momentum.

The possibility of rhythm without atmosphere: Resnais. An unpsychological way of seeing and remembering, in which the personal is entirely absorbed in the historical-allegorical, in the very age and body of the time.

Burch's point (in *Life to Those Shadows*) is that the articulation of space in the film image is grounded, centered, in the body of the viewer (identified with that of the film's director), in his or her sense of left and right, front and back, and so forth. It is grounded, let us say, in a *possible* body.

What is cinematic has to do with the penetration and articulation of space. That is, with a manifold unfolding spacetime, the constellation of sequences. A movie is more or less cinematic.

(Kazan's films are intelligent and pictorially impressive from the beginning, but they only gradually become cinematic.)

The element of tensed stillness, saturated standstill, in film imagery. Motion *picture* as a kind of nearness in distance. Here is perhaps the possibility of film's aura.

Notes On Jazz

Eric Dolphy

Dolphy's playing tends toward the histrionic. To say this is no detraction—on the contrary. It is this histrionic quality that ultimately sets him apart from Charlie Parker: something outrageous in his sound, something at once playful and agonized, fierce and humorous, almost demonic—whereas Parker's playing is never demonic. Obviously, the difference has something to do with historical epoch. Bird's postwar sobriety—as a musician—contrasts with Dolphy's disciplined, ruminative reveling in excess. In other words, Dolphy's is very much a music of the Sixties. Bird basically works *within* a form, like Bach; with great evenness and sublime rubato, he rides the "groove." Having almost single-handedly cleared a field for bebop—which, it should be remembered, initially struck many as harmonically and rhythmically bizarre—he proceeded, with sovereign assurance and unending inventiveness, to mine the emergent possibilities, producing a long string of gems. Within the riff space of bebop, he found ever new prospects for reshaping his phrase. Dolphy, on the other hand, more in the mold of Beethoven, was always restlessly pushing up against established boundaries, negotiating the uncertain, and such knowing commerce with the inchoate—"I keep hearing something else beyond what I've done" (cited in the original liner notes to *Far Cry* [1960])—makes itself felt in everything he plays. This essentially experimental impulse in his music, manifest in both its violence and its burlesque, marks it as an expression of the

Sixties-modernism, and it was no doubt what made him anathema to more than one club owner and producer, despite his personal gentleness.

Of course, the *similarities* to Parker remain: the big sound and shattering attack, the volubility and long intricate lines, the use of sometimes stark contrast as a structuring device, the fusion of virtuoso technique and raw emotion into high drama, the deep blues feeling, the tendency to play well ahead of the beat, and, finally, the incorporation of paralyzing velocity into all aspects of the musical line, of the "story," so that rapid multi-note passages have a function beyond mere underlining or filler, and speed of articulation, explicit and implicit, determines a new shock-informed melody, beyond what can be sung.[10] The diversity, even discontinuity of Bird's phrasing—André Hodeir speaks of his "piecemeal method of phrasing"—is a sign of its modernism: melody is given the stamp of montage. And Dolphy takes this tendency to an extreme. His solos typically have a kaleidoscopic quality, a little like Cecil Taylor's; they

---

10 Trumpeter Harold Baker comments on Parker's speed: "He would run through sixteenths and thirty-second notes like a tornado and then he'd come right back to loafing .... I never heard anybody play so fast. It was so fast the drummer was playing two beats. But fast as it was, it was clean, just like he was explaining to you while he was talking to somebody else." Cited in Robert Reisner, *Bird: The Legend of Charlie Parker* (1962; rpt. New York: Da Capo, 1975), p. 35. Martin Williams quotes a statement by Dolphy indicating how important this aspect of Bird's playing was to him: "I went to school with Hampton Hawes, and he was the first to tell me about Bird. I didn't believe him at first. I couldn't believe anybody could be *faster* than Hawkins, for one thing." "Introducing Eric Dolphy," in *Jazz Panorama*, ed. Williams (New York: Collier, 1962), p. 282. A consummate example of Dolphy's summoning extreme velocity for melodic purposes is his alto solo on Mal Waldron's "Fire Waltz," as performed at the Five Spot on July 16, 1961 (*Complete Prestige Recordings*, 1995).

are full of sudden interruptions, transitions, or intersections, stark antiphony often within the smallest of spaces, adumbrations of directions not pursued, all of which makes for greatly enhanced plasticity. Musical logic becomes a matter of the (explosive or implosive) interplay of sounding and moving figures—what Jack Cooke calls "collage technique" ("Eric Dolphy," *Jazz Monthly* [January 1966], p. 26). Dolphy may appear to sacrifice dignity and even rationality in the construction of his lines and may sound, in comparison to Bird, uninhibited. His music is certainly more dire. His blues are more desperate, his lyricism more on edge, just as his intervals are wider, his rhythms more disjointed, and his harmonies consequently more abrasive or surreal. But he shares with Bird a fundamental voraciousness: he could never play a tune without wholly devouring it, as he in turn was devoured by the music. They both burnt themselves out.

The *difference* from Parker is sometimes rather loosely described in terms of "expressionism." The rubric is quite apt. Think back to the high tide of European Expressionism, around 1912: Kafka's "Metamorphosis," Schiele's drawings, Schoenberg's "Pierrot Lunaire." What such works have in common is, first of all, a certain wry *distortion* of classical design, making for a certain tragicomic tone. Dolphy was fond of invoking Schoenberg. "In conversations with Eric, Schoenberg is a name that will come up frequently" (cited in Simosko and Tepperman, *Eric Dolphy: A Musical Biography*, rev. ed. [New York: Da Capo, 1996], p. 12; see also the liner notes to *Out There* on CD [1982]). Schoenberg's problem, we might say, was to discover the possibility of melody—a necessarily strange, *fremde Melodie* (the phrase is from "Pierrot")—through a medium in which the distinction between consonance and dissonance has been abolished. For Schoenberg in his expressionist period, the traditional is reborn in nontraditional space and time, necessarily transformed, generating a new set of forms that are all the more expressive, indeed virile, for being jagged and fragmentary—shock-informed. Which did not prevent his music from being *danced to* at Cabaret Voltaire in Zurich circa 1916. In other words, the intimate dismemberment the music performs on itself is actually the sublimation of a new body of primally energetic, densely textured, and richly colored sound. Thus, in his essay on Schoenberg in *Prisms*, Adorno presents the composer as supremely melodic, and Berg could speak of Schoenbergian bel canto. What this proves is that melody is an expandable concept,[11] and is not necessarily tied to tonality. Any more than beauty is necessarily tied to symmetry. What Dolphy heard in Schoenberg, Berg, and Webern, presumably has to do with their revolutionary approach to melody, as well as their conception of variegated dynamic unity, not architectonic like Bach's conception of unity but transformational, a unity-in-multiplicity involving continual quick changes of expression according to a logic of "resemblance," a kind of montage of attractions. "Pierrot Lunaire," in particular, with its irony and morbidity and delicacy and savagery, its motley fabric of moods stretched over a void, would have afforded the example of a baldly histrionic expressionism—rigorous

---

11 See Edward W. Said, *Musical Elaborations* (New York: Columbia University Press, 1991), pp. 94-96.

musical *Schauspielerei* signifying the mastering of shock. The jarring intervals that are typical of Schoenberg's compositions after 1908, and that help to give his music that air of having just arrived from another galaxy, must have had a decisive influence on Dolphy. And, though carefully distinguished from "song," Schoenberg's idea of *Sprechmelodie* (spoken melody) perhaps has a bearing on the searing and subtle instrumental vocalizations, that nakedness of voice in Dolphy's music (for which a more immediate source is of course Ornette Coleman). In Schoenberg, at any rate, the avant-garde jazzman had a model of highly refined technical knowledge married to the wildest and most somber passion. The more "cerebral" the music became, the more visceral it could be.

"Atonal jazz" was a term bandied about in the critical debates of the early Sixties, along with terms like "the new thing" and "space music." (See Martin Williams, liner notes to the George Russell Sextet, *Ezz-thetics* [1961].) Gunther Schuller's atonal, serial composition "Abstraction," into which Dolphy's playing boldly integrates itself, might serve as an example. Nevertheless, even in his furthest-out improvisations, it can be heard that Dolphy keeps touch with traditional tonality, although by 1960, if not earlier, he was no longer so at home in tonality as Parker had still been.

Between August of 1958 and June 1964, Dolphy's playing evidently underwent a significant development. One need only compare his work on something like "It Don't Mean a Thing," from Chico Hamilton's 1958 *Original*

Ellington Suite (Dolphy's first recorded solos[12]), with his work on Mingus's "Fables of Faubus," as recorded live in Stuttgart on April 28, 1964, two months before his death in Berlin, to get a sense of the distance traveled in those six years. At stake was the expressionist transcendence (not abandonment) of bebop, a process in which the bass clarinet—whose normal octave range he extended and whose outlandish sonic possibilities he never ceased to explore—played a central role. Dolphy in effect discovered the bass clarinet for jazz, and it became the medium of his most radical innovations. Already by 1960, his solos on this temperamental instrument sounded like nothing else in the world of jazz, although now and then one could hear in them echoes, perhaps, of a Jimmy Noone in the lower-register lucubrations or a Pee Wee Russell in the "dirty" sound, just as one could hear, behind the Parker influence, echoes of New Orleans and the swing era, especially Johnny Hodges, in his alto playing. (In other words, his is a rooted radicalism.) There are two recordings of Dolphy's winsome composition "Serene," from August and December 1960, that illustrate what is involved in his development, specifically in the evolving conception on bass clarinet. In a sense, what we have are two interwoven tendencies present from the beginning, one pointing backward in time, the other forward, with the latter coming to predominate; the question is a little perplexed because there are dazzling freewheeling achievements all along the way, and not every group

---

12   A recently issued amateur recording of Dolphy and Clifford Brown, with members of the latter's group, in a practice session at Dolphy's backyard studio in Los Angeles in 1954 holds no surprises, showing Dolphy in rousing and completely composed Parkeresque form.

context was favorable to experimentation. On the first recording of "Serene," for the album *Out There*, Dolphy's lines, though utterly distinctive in their mimetic power, are closer to bebop, of which he always showed himself a master (for, to the end, he remained capable of playing straight-on his brand of harmonically altered hard bop—especially on alto). A simple blues phrase, at the outset of his solo, quickly ramifies, and the bop or metabop line continually breaks up into myriad figures at varying tempos, only to reassert itself with perfect balance each time. Dolphy struts a bit, reaches into a rhapsodic upper register, and sustains a lyric vibrato. On the second recording, from the classic *Far Cry* date (CD edition), his playing bears rather less resemblance to bebop in the established sense, and the vibrato is all but gone. His solo begins with a quite different set of figures, equally bluesy, and his phrasing throughout is more surprising—precisely by reason of the heightened histrionics. Breakneck runs alternate with high-pitched, high-tension cries and brief exclamations, with sudden intimations of serenity, sometimes gloating, entailing a tumble into a chortling chalumeau. He croaks, oinks, screeches, and wheezes, and outsasses his solo of four months earlier. In other words, he further exploits the vocalistic-coloristic possibilities of the bass clarinet—opening the door to such as Steve Lacy later in the decade—and thereby expands the concept of melody. Overall, this second recording of "Serene" has a denser texture as a result of the addition of piano and trumpet. It's the wily and incisive and infinitely resourceful comping of pianist Byard, in particular, that gives the piece a transformed rhythmic feel. Byard sets off the complications, contortions, and displacements of Dolphy's line at every turn, and his solo, together with that of Booker Little, complements the ebullience of Dolphy's phrasing with concentrated, elliptical melodic explorations. For both Byard and Little were great melodists in their own right, though neither followed Dolphy into the shadows of the funhouse.

Dolphy could play a kind of earthy-spacy gospel on bass clarinet, as witness his solos on Coltrane's "Spiritual," especially the long version recorded on November 5, 1961, at the Village Vanguard, with the magisterial tenor solo preceding it. In the interview given to *Downbeat* in April of the following year, Coltrane commented on Dolphy's contribution: "A few months ago Eric was in New York, where the group was working …. So I told him to come on down and play, and he did—and turned us all around …. He'd found another way to express the same thing we had found one way to do" ("John Coltrane and Eric Dolphy Answer the Jazz Critics," April 12, 1962).

Coltrane had a part in the developing expansiveness of Dolphy's playing. Listen to Dolphy's stretched-out treatment of "Softly, As In a Morning Sunrise," in *The Illinois Concert* of March 1963, a bass clarinet solo and reprise that show the influence of Coltrane and contrast strikingly to the concentrated Parkeresque treatment of this tune on alto two years earlier, with a group led by Ron Carter on the album *Where?*.

Dolphy's talents as a composer—in the tradition of Parker, Monk, and Mingus—are on display in the Alfred Lion-produced studio recording of February 25, 1964,

Out to Lunch, with its celebrated ensemble work. This album also contains what is perhaps the most perfect and most eloquent set of Dolphy solos ever recorded. All three of his instruments are heard at their most "advanced," and the intensity level of his playing (a function, naturally, of the group context) is nowhere greater. At the same time, an introspective, an interrogatory and meditative mood pervades this sustained collective improvisation, tempering the element of outcry, occasionally frantic, in Dolphy's playing. The bass clarinet solo on "Hat and Beard"—the title refers to the image of Monk—is a masterpiece of "talking" jazz, expressive of the permutations of talk; the solo is full of vividly contrasting, diversely inflected figures—ranging in expression from the urgent to the quizzical, the gazelle-like to the mastodonic—and yet it is unified dramatically. What Monk thinks of as story form ("when it begins to tell a story, when it gets a certain *sound*") has in large part superseded traditional chorus improvisation here, with a gain in immediacy as well as amplitude. To be sure, there is no lack of rhythmic and harmonic constraints: "every note I play has some reference to the chords of the piece" (quoted in *Eric Dolphy: A Musical Biography*, p. 11). Moreover, a bebop pattern is implied throughout, if almost never stated—a procedure reminiscent, once again, of Monk. In fact, with all of Dolphy's solos on *Out to Lunch*, the bebop line persists as a kind of virtual substrate, out of which arises the carnival of figures. Multi-note runs form long angular phrases, the proliferating individual notes effectively melded in white heat, as is sometimes the case in Parker's solos. And just as Parker has a way of coming to the surface in a flowering of lyric simplicity before diving back down into the complexities (for example, "All the Things You Are," as performed at the Massey Hall concert in 1953), so Dolphy intersperses his magnificent alto solo on the Monkish "Straight Up and Down" with variously charged, pulsating silences, like eyes in a storm. Hence, at his furthest remove from conventional bebop, he maintains a nearness to its origins.

Jaki Byard on Dolphy's relation to Parker: "It's interesting that, although he's got so much of his own going, Eric is the only one of all the cats who's captured Bird's *true* tone" (quoted by Michael Cuscuna, 1970, in liner notes to *Far Cry*). This echoes Mingus's judgment: "He doesn't sound a thing like Ornette Coleman. He phrases more like Bird. And he has absorbed Bird rhythmically" (cited in Williams, "Introducing Eric Dolphy," *Jazz Panorama*, p. 283). But one should not discount the Coleman influence: "[Ornette] taught me a direction"—so Dolphy claimed in 1960 (Williams, "Vintage Dolphy," in *Jazz Changes* [New York: Oxford Univ. Press, 1992], p. 225).

Parker: "If you don't live it, it won't come out of your horn" (the oft-quoted line from Ross Russell, *Bird Lives!* [1973; rpt. New York: Da Capo, 1996], p. 293). It might be said of Parker that the dionysian character of his life took apollonian form in his art.

In his liner notes to *Far Cry*, Cuscuna remarks that "Dolphy always gets a leaping, stretching effect out of his melodies. Byard explained that 'that particular flavor he gets in his originals comes from the fact that he uses the upper structure of the chords—raised ninths, flatted thirteenths, etc.'" This too has a precedent in Parker:

"One night I was jamming in a chili house," recalls Bird, "on Seventh Avenue …. It was December, 1939. Now I'd been getting bored with the stereotyped changes … and I kept thinking there's bound to be something else. I could hear it sometimes, but I couldn't play it. Well, that night, I was working over 'Cherokee,' and, as I did, I found that by using the higher intervals of a chord as a melody line and backing them with appropriately related changes, I could play the thing I'd been hearing. I came alive" (quoted in Reisner, *Bird: The Legend of Charlie Parker*, p. 239).

The pronounced physicality of Dolphy's sound: another component in his constructive destruction of bebop. The animality of that sound. In the case of the flute, on which he always stayed closer to bop, there were the lessons not just of the Bird but of birds, which he liked to talk about to interviewers. In the short trio section—flute, piano, and bass—toward the end of Mingus's "Meditations for Integration," on the glorious *Live in Paris* recording of April 17, 1964, we hear indications, mournful and sardonic, of what might have happened on flute had his career not been cut short—indications pointing in the direction of transformed sonority, obedient to the breath of the music. (He spoke, intriguingly, of working up his alto flute).

The quirky "conversation" with Mingus toward the end of the Stuttgart "Fables of Faubus": an apotheosis of the histrionic. Not only ornithology but zoology and phantomology. Mingus, in the dominant role, a little prolix and insistent in laying down the line. Dolphy (on bass clarinet) more childlike, amazed, yet skeptical and melancholy mad, making pointed remarks that trail off into silence and raising delicate, sometimes painful questions that provoke the bass to further demonstrations. As a leader, Mingus cultivated his own strain of tragi-clownish histrionics in which Dolphy was obviously at home. In the summer and fall of 1960, playing with the Mingus Jazz Workshop, Dolphy gets pretty far "outside," and the musical confabulation with his old friend on bass recorded October 20 ("What Love?") is so full of variety as to constitute a full-fledged scene at the crossroads of humor, bathos and rage. Dolphy's sound is uncannily *loosed*—in effect, ventriloquizing.

The triumphant "Stormy Weather" on alto with Mingus, from the session recorded October 20, 1960. The classicism in Dolphy's modernism is nowhere clearer.

For sheer drama: the alto solo on "Mendacity" (Max Roach, *Percussion Bitter Sweet*, 1961).

Dolphy listened hard to Cecil Taylor's records. "I think I'm learning how to play with Cecil" (quoted in A. B. Spellman, *Four Lives in the Bebop Business* [New York: Limelight, 1966], p. 15). A deep-rooted affinity, a study that absorbed him, an inspiration, a future that went unrealized. Coming from the most relentlessly antilyrical of the jazz modernists, Taylor's formula "Sing it!" could serve as an epitaph for Dolphy.

STEVE LACY

Steve Lacy quotes Thelonious Monk on the latter's method of excavating a tune: "You've got to dig it to dig it, you dig it?"[13] For it was a dictum of the great pianist that the inside of a tune is what makes the outside sound good. Monk's way of paralyzing a familiar melody—unstringing its phrases and letting fragmentary riffs or even single notes resonate uncannily or shatter into multi-colored particles—served as model for Lacy's minimalism, what he called his materialist investigations. "Space," he said of Monk, "he's into space." By which he meant an essentially *plastic* articulation of the musical problematic, a configured, constellatory rather than prevailingly linear way of thinking and proceeding, so as in effect to carve musical space. "He could make sounds that were just like jewels." Although Monk was there on 52nd Street, with Parker and Gillespie and Powell, at the beginnings of bebop, and was indeed the brains of the bebop revolution and the resident guru for the younger players like Cecil Taylor and Lacy himself, he was also a decisive counterforce to the bop "athleticism" (Lacy's term), the rigorous, high-velocity technique of running the changes on a chord structure, often with little relation to the melody of the piece. Originally, the athleticism was integral to the musical statement; the sensation of supersonic velocity in a solo by Charlie Parker was a

---

13   "In the Old Days," a 1997 interview with Steve Lacy, in *Steve Lacy: Conversations*, ed. Jason Weiss (Durham, NC: Duke University Press, 2006), p. 201. Unless otherwise indicated, all quotations of Lacy in the text are from this book.

matter not just of the great number of notes played in quick succession but of the concentration and explosiveness of the phrasing, which of course balanced the cool.

Bebop music was a baroque development of the high-speed syncopations that distinguished jazz from the beginning, and it had all the direness of the baroque. Monk's accentuation of the music was jagged and precipitous compared to Bird's or Miles' line; without abandoning the new dissonant harmonies of bebop, in fact enriching them, he opened up spaces for melodic exploration or for "telling a story," as he liked to put it, and consequently slowed the music down. More precisely, he *implies* bebop acceleration at every turn while deconstructing the bebop grid. And in thus "getting down," he flavors the direness with a pervasive sense of the comic. No less imbued than Monk was with every era of the music's development, from New Orleans to Kansas City, Lacy too opened up new spaces for jazz composition and improvisation through his own monkish—that is, aphoristic—melodic radicalism and his own broad and brooding and whimsical, even cartoonish, sense of humor (all of this fully evident in the classic 1963 live recording *School Days*, with its consummate collective improvisation of Monk's music). Crucial to the digging and transplanting of roots was his self-imposed exile from New York in the late Sixties, at a time when jazz, as a distinctly American art form, seemed to have exhausted its resources and lost its audience. Lacy's long and varied encounter with European and Asian musicians—which continued even after his triumphant return to America in 2002, two years before his death—represents, we can see now, a new awakening and cosmopolitan transformation of the tradition of Louis Armstrong and Duke Ellington.

Already in 1961, with the Ellington-Strayhorn composition "Something to Live For," on the album *Evidence*, co-led with his "brother" Don Cherry, one can hear a breakthrough quality announcing itself in Lacy's solo along with the characteristic laconism that allows us to feel what he has learned to leave out. I'm referring to the unobtrusive but decisive critical edge that gives his musical voice its signature lucid and unrhetorical idiomaticity (see Nat Hentoff's liner notes to the album) and its gravity. Nothing arbitrary or factitious—that was his motto. And nothing stale. It's as if, in this moment-to-moment recursive vigilance, making for a virtually composite mode of construction, he shifts perspective a little with every phrase, so that each move and each elegant or disconcerting transition brings about an unexpected melodic inflection, as if the song were constantly beginning anew in musical metamorphosis.

That Lacy's extended, intermittent leave, starting in 1965, from song form and conventional harmony may have had an enriching effect on what was from the first an inimitable way with a song is suggested by his rendition of the three poignant Mingus compositions, in duet with his old friend and mentor Gil Evans, on *Paris Blues* (1987). In this unfailingly intelligent collaboration, recorded in Paris near the end of Evans's life, the *magic* that was the conscious, if elusive, goal of these two master technicians was very much in evidence. Lacy's return to song here attests, in the sovereign assurance of his arcing lines as much as the extraordinary subtlety of his vibrato, in all the warmth and austerity of expression, to the wilds traversed.

The Beat Suite (2001): the art song makes a legitimate, a truly original and exultant entry into jazz, with unprecedented textures and colors, and all simultaneous or converging musical events emerging as melodies. The compositional power—Lacy's compositions are generally characterized by a combination of buoyancy and relentlessness—and the group dynamic are perhaps at their height in the pieces devoted to works by Burroughs, Kaufman, Waldman, and Rexroth. But the album as a whole, with the "poly-free" correspondence of these uniquely seasoned individual voices (and this time perhaps the trombone and bass above all), is ripe for rediscovery.

"Why did you choose the soprano?" "I fell in love with it…above all, because of its sound" (interview in *Jazz Magazine*, August 1965). Just as Eric Dolphy single-handedly retrieved the bass clarinet for modern jazz, Steve Lacy retrieved the soprano saxophone.

As the school of modern dance has drawn inspiration from "natural movement," from walking or falling, or from the swinging shut of a door, so Lacy has learned from bird calls or the sound of rain or the sound of footsteps, or from the mistakes made by amateurs with whom he sometimes plays. He likes to talk about "material" (using the Italian slang word *roba*), meaning not just musical ideas proper but an evolving repertory of interrelated sonic, textural, structural possibilities, in part elicited from material objects and their intersection, and from various everyday milieux and traffic jams. Sound collage: "knitting needles, ashtrays, keys, finger snapping, loose change, and also silence." It was the voice in and of the material itself, lurking in the walls and corners or right behind the furniture, "the music that's hidden," that he was after. With his musical associates he conducted multi-faceted researches into the densities of the "cryptosphere." An exemplary, that is, singular fruit of these bold and patient experimental soundings—reminiscent perhaps of the Dolphy-Mingus colloquies of the mid-Sixties—is the 1978 collaboration with Dutch bassist Maarten Altena, *High, Low and Order*, and especially the final piece "Kiss."

The sounds he got from the soprano saxophone! He would listen to the horn as he played—striving, as he put it, to let the music play him—and try to work out the implications of what he heard, try to trace the story-elements or the geometries adumbrated, however fleetingly, and bring out the color combinations, not forgetting to take into account the environing situation. It had to do, in essence, with avoiding "the bad habit of thinking in terms of chords." He didn't want to bore himself.

He liked to play with musicians who were "stronger" than he was—Cecil Taylor or Archie Shepp, Misha Mengelberg or the saxophonist Steve Potts. They took off, and he could never catch up. It inspired him to surpass himself. By "stronger" he doesn't exactly mean "better." It's a matter of athleticism, or virility, which can be good or bad.

Stronger—as a force of nature may be stronger than you. Some players are monsters.

The majestic duet with Roswell Rudd on "Pannonica," recorded in Montreal in April 1992 (at a much slower tempo than that of the trio version on *School Days*), brings out— along with the winsome and the tender—a tragicomic feeling in Monk's tribute to the jazz baroness, his patroness and Lacy's friend.[14] Seven years later, together with Rudd, Avenel, and Betsch on Lacy's often-performed composition "The Bath" (*Monk's Dream*), it is tenderness married to burlesque (shades of Dicky Wells!).

Many instruments, he once said, are slumbering within the soprano saxophone. This makes it particularly treacherous to play, aside from the well-known difficulties it presents for intonation. (In the 1985 documentary film *Steve Lacy: Lift the Bandstand*, directed by Peter Bull, he compares the horn to a shrill, unruly and ungrateful child, one given to hysterics; it always needs to be cooled down and tamed.) In addition to various woodwinds, brasses, and stringed instruments, Lacy's soprano— this is its mimetic grandeur—could sound like several different species of feathered or furry creature, natural phenomena like winds and breezes, bubbling streams or digestion, mechanical apparatuses modern and primordial, spectral presences or banshee wails, and above all

---

14 "[T]he jazz baroness, Nica Koenigswarter, who was a dear friend,...helped me get the gig with Thelonious in 1960" (liner notes to *Monk's Dream*). Lacy worked with Monk for sixteen weeks at the Jazz Gallery in New York in 1960, after first hearing him play in 1955. He recorded with Monk on the latter's *Big Band and Quartet in Concert* (1963), and he can be heard, sounding somewhat constrained, with Monk's quartet in a radio broadcast from 1960, now on the CD *Thelonious Monk in Philadelphia 1960 With Steve Lacy* and on the 2011 reissue of *School Days*. The 1992 duet with Rudd is included on the CD *Associates*.

the human voice, indeed the different registers and consistencies of the female voice.

And then there is "The Whammies," as recorded with trombonist George Lewis in Paris in 1982 (*Associates*): the panoply of sounds from the two instruments has the feel of a radio show originating from a distant galaxy strangely like our own.

Lacy's work with Cecil Taylor from 1953 to 1959, though publicly it involved a lot of dance jobs, encouraged an antilyrical lyricism, a certain wild analytic that nevertheless swings. "What I learned from Cecil Taylor," he commented at the beginning of 2004, "is about language and structure." Exposing the fundamentals, as the cubists liked to do, made new creation possible. And not least, in this case, new sonorities. It was Cecil Taylor who drew him out of the New Orleans school in which he began (and with which he would never lose touch[15]) into the ocean of the avant-garde; it was Cecil who made it possible for him to discover Monk (beginning with "Bemsha Swing" and then the man himself at "a little club downtown" populated only by musicians), and who introduced him also to Merce Cunningham (the connection to dance, to the choreographic articulation of space, was always crucial), and to "Stravinsky, Bartók, and all that."[16] And it was Cecil Taylor who taught him that "jazz

---

[15] The link to Pee Wee Russell (with whom he played in the old Stuyvesant Casino in New York) is especially noteworthy; it can be felt perhaps above all in Lacy's understated and elliptical, "grey" way with the blues. He is much closer to Russell than to Sidney Bechet.

[16] See Lacy's written tribute to Stravinsky, "He Flew" (1980), in *Steve Lacy: Conversations*, pp. 253-255: "[E]verything he did was dance.... I think what made Stravinsky the man of his century is

is political," that its voice is dissident, or better be, however popular its appeal.

Cecil Taylor's spirit, nourished on Schoenberg as much as on Ellington, Monk, and Bud Powell, can be felt presiding over the collaboration with the great Belgian pianist Fred Van Hove at Berlin's Akademie der Künste in April 1996 (*Five Facings*). Their twenty-minute free improvisation "Twenty One" manifests a perfect integration not only of sound-effects into musical discourse but of the American avant-garde into the European. Lacy's duet encounters are rarely, I daresay, as "far out" and yet intimately attuned as this one is. The interplay is truly uncanny, and it yields high drama.

Lacy's vast discography bears witness to the fact that he liked playing with the same musicians over time. The hard-won sense of community, the evolving cross fertilization, made it possible for the individual players to explore and take risks, while together maintaining an "organic" continuity in discontinuity. For the danger was "dryness." It could happen that someone not familiar with his playing would sometimes mistake his divagations for being lost and consequently become lost himself. The music for Lacy was nothing if not a continual learning experience.

As "training," he would transcribe Webern's pieces for soprano voice in order to play them on his saxophone. He was interested in what the late composer was doing with song form and cadence, the brevity and the density of these lieder, the rhythmic displacement ("those floating

---

that he arrived at a new appreciation of the raw material of sound."

rhythms") and prismatic sense of space, the dynamics and slow tempos, "the specificity of it all." During the straight-ahead Fifties, he remarked in a 2002 interview, everybody he knew was listening to Webern.

As for dynamics as a structural principle, listen to Lacy's work with Japanese percussionist Masahiko Togashi—for example, on Togashi's composition "Haze," recorded in Hiroshima in 1983 (*Associates*)—or to the unadorned "free jazz" album, *The Forest and the Zoo*, recorded in concert in Buenos Aires in 1966.

It was not a question of beauty in any conventional sense (though he would talk about "proportion," "purity," "economy," and especially—sometimes referring to the work of Klee or Cézanne—"plasticity"), any more than it was a question of technique in itself (the better-trained you are, he would say, the more traps there are to fall into). The keen, alternately full-bodied and shrunken animality of the sound, the constantly modulating histrionics, just as much as the variable appropriation of speech rhythms and phraseology, served the goal of "life." The only criterion for the music was: is it alive or dead? That meant maintaining an edge, an opening to the unknown, a more or less emphatically interrogatory mood. But the experimental initiative, in turn, could only prove fruitful if it was allied to the most rigorous discipline and to experiential knowledge. The quartet with Roswell Rudd, Henry Grimes, and Dennis Charles in the early Sixties spent many months "underground" getting every measure of Monk's challenging music precisely right (as measured by the records rather than by written scores) before taking the leap beyond certainty into improvisational "freedom." The schooling in structure and detail was necessary if they were to get "inside"—to dig—each particular tune in its nexus of possibilities and, through this nightly mining of the musical problematic before audiences in clubs and coffee houses, to bring about the spontaneous, measured rapprochement of improvisation and composition. Only such collective immersion in the material could make them feel secure enough to drop the security in their playing and attain real authority. That was the beauty of it. "It's all in the cooking."

Pee Wee Russell

The whole history of the music resonates in its greatest moments.

Pee Wee Russell's solos with Monk at Newport in 1963 are, one may say, more truly Monkish in spirit than sideman Charlie Rouse's hard-bop solos preceding them. On the first tune, "Nutty," after a shattering statement by Rouse that no-one would want to follow, Pee Wee comes on in the most unprepossessing, spare sort of way but builds—with gravelly blues feeling, and an inimitable melancholy insouciance that can suddenly turn savage, or acid—builds triumphantly on the melody he has transformed, tells a story with it as Monk would expect, and opens up a new world of his own. His lines are memorable in a way that Rouse's more technically elaborate lines are not.

Without playing a great many notes, Russell suggests or obliquely cites the bebop velocity in a manner not dissimilar to Monk's own eccentric swing. (Sidemen Warren and Dunlop really dig what he does.)

And their sense of humor unites them. Monk audibly chuckles at an especially quizzical and sour turn of phrase in Pee Wee's solo on "Blue Monk."

BEBOP PIANO

MONK

Against the bebop velocity Monk's retarding movement—his spaced-out phraseology— yields greater suddenness. Vortical lines of questioning, explosive rejoinders, mournful and jubilant tracery across the void. (Louis Armstrong's vocals.) Bebop velocity is always implicit in Monk's playing, though *almost* never stated.

In Monk any remaining trace of the gorgeous, such as often predominates in Powell (not to mention Tatum), subserves a ruthlessly parodic end.

In terms of sound and color, Monk's most important predecessor is doubtless Ellington, in terms of rhythm and accent arguably Basie. At the origin of his modernism is a certain stride. Eccentric stride.

It was Monk who first broke through the methodology of bebop; his new chords and new rhythms arise as a solution to the problems of bebop. His development is marked by the increasingly complex play of sonorities, though melody for him is from the beginning a function of unfolding sonority. There is an extraordinary sourness in the tonality of late Monk.

"Jackie-ing" from ca. 1965 (*April in Paris*): Monk at his funniest. Unearthly beams of funk at the end of his solo and in accompaniment to Gales' eloquent bass. Harshness and humor—"Get *down*!"

Late Monk: practically every note is a pane of glass in a structure of great arch. Virtually no embellishment, for *all* is ornament in transition.

It is old wisdom, of course, that melody is enriched by the possibilities of dissonance. In improvisatory music, the risk of the false note contributes to the quality of the sound.

"He was ... very interested in errors, and when someone made a mistake he would pick up on it and examine the *ramifications* (Duke's word) therein" (Steve Lacy on Monk, preface to Thomas Fitterling, *Thelonious Monk: His Life and Music*, trans. R. Dobbin [Berkeley, 1997], p. 12).

Parker's resistance to Monk—like that of Miles later on—was at times savage. But what made Bird great, and *linked* him to Monk, was his sense of drama, something at times totally absent in Diz's solos, sophisticated as they usually are.

Whereas Bill Evans would sit hunched over the piano keys, sunken and immobilized in study, Monk would almost tumble off the bench in the violence of his attack. What most distinguishes Evans from Monk is not the former's "lyricism" (which could be highly astringent) but the latter's angularity. What's Monkish is spaced out.

Monk's method of fragmenting a melody ("The Man I Love," with Miles, first take).

Monk's relation to Tatum is like Fosse's relation to Astaire.

"[Monk] doesn't have any [technique], just for what he does he has. He used to kind of skidder-over, like an ice skater, over an Art Tatum-like run; he never really made the whole thing, but he made the shape of it and the time .... I think that he probably never learned how to finger pianistically correctly. So he made his own way.

But it was quite an influence" (Johnny Carisi, quoted in *Swing to Bop*, ed. Ira Gitler [New York, 1985], p. 102).

"If you listen to Monk's sounds and his rhythm, then you can still hear that old sanctified influence" (Jackie McLean, *Four Lives in the Bebop Business*, compiled by A.B. Spellman [New York, 1966], p. 201).

"The intellectuals in Greenwich village [in the late Forties] sneered at what they considered Monk's primitive technique" (Fitterling, p. 44). They had no ear for the knowing naïve.

Mary Lou Williams and others have testified that Monk's unusual harmonic flavor was already evident in the mid-Thirties (when he was traveling with the sanctified band). But the fact remains that, as far as the recorded output goes, his harmonies are generally more dissonant, as his rhythms are more jagged, after 1956.

Monk came into fashion in 1958-1959 (*Downbeat* Critics' Award). "Jackie-ing" composed in 1959.

Herbie Nichols, in an early review (1946), referred to Monk's "magnificent melodic lines" (Fitterling, p. 37).

The long, interrupted "'Round Midnight" on *Thelonious Himself* (1957): splendid and splenetic. The aporias mostly mark the starting of untoward questions, the points at which improvisation broaches mistake, and melodic-harmonic breakthrough becomes breakdown. ("Remarkable how Monk always managed to explore radically new territory when playing this, his most famous piece" [Fitterling, p. 168]).

Gigi Gryce is one of the few horn players whose melodic imagination is nearly as rapid, flexible and lucid, if not so profound, as Monk's own, and that's why their

1955 collaboration on *Nica's Tempo* is such a gem. Standing out is the almost fretful "Gallop's Gallop" and the almost jaunty "Brake's Sake," with the broken phrasing in the solos.

A commonplace in jazz: *what* you say is critical, but the artistry is in the *how*.

Melody a function of sound and story: "When it begins to tell a story, when it gets a certain *sound*, then the thing clicks—the interpretation is perfect" (Monk, quoted in Fitterling, p. 68). In other words, musical statement is not based first of all on instrumental facility. What finally matters in improvising is not "technique" per se but knowledge, or rather thinking. Exercise of the musical problematic.

Monk: it is not a matter of left hand versus right, but of incorporating dissonances into the melodic line itself.

On the whole, the most interesting jazz pianists are Monk-spawned.

POWELL

It has been suggested that Monk passed on to Powell both his music and his madness. "Monk wrote for Bud. All his music was written for Bud Powell ..., because he figured Bud was the only one who could play it" (Kenny Clarke, in *Swing to Bop*, p. 102).

Among boppers, none with deeper blues feeling than Bud Powell. "He outbirded Bird and he outdizzied Dizzy" (Al Haig on Powell, in *Swing to Bop*, p. 102).

By May 1958, when he recorded with the two Jones's in an atmosphere as charged with intensity as it was palpably relaxed, the gorgeous (the Tatumesque) was gone from Powell's playing, while the density and dissonance (the Monkish) was in its glory.

The new CD sets make it evident that the record companies generally passed over the darker, more dissonant material recorded by Powell, preferring to market the gorgeous.

— Epitome of the gorgeous: "Autumn in New York" (8/14/53). Entirely commercial. — The gorgeous subjected to dissonance, retarded gorgeous: "My Devotion" (9/53).

Powell's kitsch ("Glass Enclosure") is more grand than that of, say, Gene DiNovi in the Nineties ("It Never Entered My Head").

The chuckles and grunts of his mates as Bud makes unexpected moves ("Buster Rides Again"). Surprise is, after all, a hallmark of what Baudelaire called "modern beauty." Tired playing: not much is left unsaid.

Cecil Taylor on Powell: "the real thing of Bud, with

all the physicality of it, with the filth of it, and the movement in the attack" (*Four Lives in the Bebop Business*, p. 62).

Though many imitated his style, no one could punctuate like Powell.

Speed in jazz, if it is to be meaningful, is not something simply quantitative, not just a function of the number of notes played in succession, but also a matter of how you cut into the line. It is a matter of making quick moves in the context of a whole conception, a whole sounding and moving spacetime. Jazz and film: reveling in speed.

Velocity and the retarding principle: speeding up and speeding down. The danger in bebop is that velocity can become an end in itself (as happens sometimes in Kenny Drew and others). Listen to the way Powell alternately drags behind the beat, gravitating expansively, and wells ahead of it.

The bebop direness, the resistance to lyricism, the lyrical friction.

TWARDZIK

No one else can quite propagate a rhythm, while paralyzing it, as Richard Twardzik does. His playing has an almost unprecedented range of lyric expression along with a suddenness of transition. He fleers and gibes, is puckish and satanic (e.g., with Serge Chaloff). Together with unabashed joy, one hears ironized solitude and death in virtually everything he plays.

Twardzik's conception is more "pianistic" and perhaps more various than that of Monk, who no doubt paved the way for him. Like Thelonious, he brings out the parodic nature of jazz. They are both interested in opening up the harmonic-rhythmic spaces of bebop.

But while Twardzik's solos as sideman (with Parker, Mariano, Chaloff, Baker) are often shattering, the music on the one album he led is occasionally ponderous—perhaps overrehearsed. Or playing too much to the white audience (for whom the "heart attack at age 24" was fabricated).

Paris, October 1955. "Everyone showed up [in the recording studio] but Dick [who, we hear a page earlier, was always on time and always playing exceptionally]. We waited an hour, then Peter [Littman, the drummer, and Twardzik's friend from Boston] volunteered to go to his hotel room and see what was happening. About an hour later Peter rushed into the studio completely hysterical, screaming that Dick was dead. He said that he and the hotel manager had broken the door open and found Dick bright blue, the spike still in his arm" (Chet Baker, *As Though I Had Wings* [New York: St. Martin's, 1997], p. 71.

Others talk about Twardzik's gentleness, studiousness, love of argument, perfectionism, encyclopedic memory, and absorption in music of the Baroque.

Russ Freeman was the producer of Twardzik's recording session for Pacific Records in December 1954, and he shares the billing with him on the record. In the liner notes, he mentions that he encountered the young pianist in Boston and was struck by his "uninhibited" way with harmonies, his "really original concept."

"Then there was this white cat, Dick Twardzik .... In 1955 he had destroyed some Kenton people by playing like Bud Powell first and getting them all excited and then going into his, at that time, Schoenbergian bag while they were playing Errol Garner chords. He was like the white pianist power up there .... My conception had developed by then, and while I was playing [at the Stable in Boston], Twardzik came in, and he sort of did a dance around the edge of the piano" (Cecil Taylor, as quoted in *Four Lives in the Bebop Business*, p. 59). Taylor, two years younger than Twardzik, had seen him perform in an Arts Festival on the Boston Common in the summer of 1954, where he was featured together with Martha Graham's dance company and an exhibition of abstract expressionists.

As a dancer, Twardzik is always up in the air.

Although the very usefully annotated recordings of Parker at the Hi Hat in Boston on December 14, 1952 (Uptown, 1996), make it clear that Twardzik, for all his super-speedy moves, was not a bebop player in the conventional sense (as the other pianist on this disc, the unsung Rollins Griffith, clearly was), still it can be said that he was in his element playing Parker's bubbling compositions. These six piano solos—particularly the radiant interpretation of "Don't Blame Me," which witnesses to the 21-year-old pianist's full maturity of conception—represent a creative skewing of bebop lines, and they introduce a new irridescent coloration. Following the piano solo on "Cool Blues," Parker unfolds out of Twardzik's universe.

The rumor of dissension between Twardzik and Mingus is not borne out by their recorded interplay at the Hi Hat. The piano really gets down behind the bass on "Cheryl."

The surprising is at the highest premium in Twardzik's solos.

Parker drops in unannounced at the Jazz Workshop on January 22, 1954, to play a set with Twardzik.

Twardzik's incandescent sonority goes together with rigorous construction. This is no less evident in the shorter forms, as with the crystalline introduction and coda to "Lover Man" in Stuttgart in 1955.

The Twardzik track on *The Happy Bird*, "I'll Remember April" (date unknown, reissued 1997). The barely audible, winged piano solo—its lines swift as meditation, its harmonies at once sunny and dire—is perhaps his most interesting on record, and an indication of how "far out" he could go in live performance, especially "after hours." As with Parker himself, the fiery, shimmering velocity—more suggested than delineated note for note—is perfectly integrated into the melody, which is never sentimental but rather sly and audacious at the same time. With all his quirkiness, he matches Bird's passion.

HOPE

The category of growth can be decisive in an artist. Bud Powell did not really develop. Elmo Hope did. But, from the earliest recordings on, Hope is both lighter and more somber than Powell.

The legend is that, as boys in New York, Hope and Powell spent long hours together studying recordings of classical music and woodshedding at the piano. Each was giving solo recitals by age 15.

"They're all, or nearly all, jivin'" (Hope interviewed in *Downbeat*, Jan. 5, 1961). On this same occasion he also observes: "The white musicians are better equipped to make my music. But when they get down into those changes, they're in trouble."

Hope's piano sometimes has a sound like breaking glass.

By April of '58, Hope had entered his late phase, with its discontinuous swing, at once airier and denser than what had come before. The colors are now darker and more ambiguous, the lines more jagged, the transitions more sudden and the spaces wider, the melodies more fragmented—all witnessing to a consummation of the early schooling with Monk.

The retarding principle with Hope: a whirling sphere of chromatic intimations, virtually invisible in its extreme velocity, on the surface of which are traced the simplest and most discreet lines and curves (e.g., "B's A-Plenty," 2/8/59).

Hope's subterranean influence particularly marked in the legendary Hasaan Ibn-Ali, in whom the bebop direness climaxes. Joyous dire.

NICHOLS

On eloquence in improvisation. A sensation, in listening to Nichols' music, with its oblique relation to bebop, of doors suddenly opening, one after another, on various melodic landscapes, various trains of thought—musical problems or *questions*—into one of which we have scarcely taken a step before we are tendered an invitation to another doorway opening onto another prospect, all the exfoliating spaces nonetheless cohering—strangely and quite knowingly configuring a single passageway, a continuous if elliptical discourse. It is a discourse that is never insistent, never showy, but often ironic, somber, ebullient, and often staggering in its gentleness (a supreme example is "Wildflower," with two other distinctive melodists, Teddy Kotick and Max Roach, recorded in April 1956). In other words, virtually every motivic elaboration, every turn of phrase, every shading or brightening, entails a melodic discovery, a witty intimation of possibilities raised in passing. At times, the formulation is astonishingly abbreviated, a tiny squiggle of notes, a chord merely brushed along its receding edge, a splash of color in response to a drum passage. At other times, a swift complicated run set off by a brief interval of silence. At every point, both a developing architecture—rigorous variation on the particular theme announced at the head—and aphoristic dissolution into pure expression. The logical construction sings—coolly intense, earthy and refined.

In the music of Herbie Nichols, with its harmonic roots recognizably in Monk, one nevertheless hears the whole history of jazz.

During a Greenwich Village loft benefit in 1962, Nichols played in a pick-up band that included Archie Shepp and Ahmad Abdul Malik. It was the last time he performed modern jazz—as opposed to the Dixieland by which he earned a meager living—before an audience.

Herbie Nichols: perfect balance of density and wingedness. The stillness enables the amplitude. Continuity in discontinuity of phrasing, rhythmic interruptions of the rhythm. What Roswell Rudd calls variegated harmony. All the resources of pianism and rubato in the service of highly disciplined exploration. As one might say of a graphic artist or a dancer, he has noble line.

The mysteriously shy majesty of "The Spinning Song," with its unsurpassed trio work (April 19, 1956). Music that haunts.

"There were times when I'd be playing with or listening to Herbie and I'd get the feeling he was lost, but he always knew where it was and he'd pop up and be right on track" (Danny Barker, cited in the liner notes to *The Complete Blue Note Recordings of Herbie Nichols* [Mosaic, 1987]).

At Monroe's Uptown in the late Thirties, Herbie played the music that was transitioning from swing to bebop; he played, by his own estimation, as "fast and wild as lightning" (*Four Lives in the Bebop Business*, p. 158). This is an indication of the extent of his undocumented but deducible development, of all the concentration—the sublimation of the wild—that went into the late style, where the lightning strikes intermittently, where we find the greatest possible elegance in the modulation of velocity.

"Look what a hard time bop had getting through. People who were making it off swing, like Benny Goodman [elsewhere he singles out Ellington and Basie], were able to hold it back. It was years before the bop records got through" (Nichols, quoted in *Four Lives in the Bebop Business*, p. 160).

"What are you playing, man? You sound like you're in a third world" (saxophonist Sahib Shihab to Nichols; "The Third World" is the title of a Nichols composition). "He was ghosting or acting out a lot of moves but really *sounding* only certain choice ones" (Roswell Rudd on Nichols' left hand [*Complete Blue Note Recordings*, liner notes]).

Unfolding matrix of possibilities, encompassing probability fluid, telos out of which each moment of improvisation is born.

The Bethlehem sessions (from 1957, as partially re-released in 1994) are lacking the edge of the music Nichols recorded a year-and-a-half earlier for Alfred Lion.

In 1957-58, virtually unnoticed by producers and listeners alike ("The owners used to think I was too far out" [quoted in *Four Lives in the Bebop Business*, p. 162]), Nichols was playing at the Page 3 in New York, where he sometimes accompanied Sheila Jordan on tunes like "Lush Life" and "Love for Sale." There "Monk, Randy Weston, and Cecil Taylor all came to hear Herbie. *They* knew that he was an original" (Patti Brown, cited in the liner notes to *The Complete Blue Note Recordings of Herbie Nichols*).

CECIL TAYLOR

A manner of sampling sounds (Adorno, *Quasi una Fantasia*, p. 136). Connection here with jazz piano: Cecil Taylor. This is not the same as eclecticism.

What saves Cecil Taylor in his pianistic immersion, and especially earlier on, are indefinables: his blues feeling and his sense of humor.

Cecil Taylor seeks to square the swing—by the overwhelming linearity of his approach, in which color and dynamics supersede melody as they never do in Monk. More kaleidoscopic than the boppers.

The retarding principle, in music as in poetry, is a principle of truncation and implication (*truncus*, cut short, lopped, maimed—from an Indo-European root meaning to cross over, pass through, overcome).

Taylor on playing the music: "The notes that we play are old music, man …. When you play with authority then that's what the music is about, like ooooooh baby, and sing it. You've got to hear it and these people will hear it too, if all that shit is reduced" (*Four Lives in the Bebop Business*, p. 20). On the critique of jazz by such as John Cage: "They simply don't recognize the criteria" (34).

What is thus at stake in jazz improvisation, according to Taylor, is not technique per se but "authority."

"Swinging" becomes problematic with Taylor, although at least up to a point his music remains "danceable"—and in a way not entirely unrelated perhaps to the way Schoenberg's music is danceable (Cabaret Voltaire, circa 1916). According to sideman Raphé Malik, Taylor sometimes performed with dancers.

Cecil Taylor: at the end of a phrase, his line will sometimes pulverize, colored dust motes scattered into space. As if his voice suddenly ebbed for a measure. His notes are thrown like dice, are whisked, curled, blasted, or else laid down like slabs, like granite blocks or iron grating. Metallic. At once delicate and massive.

In his solos on the 1958 recording with Coltrane, he will swallow, voraciously, the end of a phrase, infinitely expanding the element of the unexpected that Powell made so important. These solos, despite his own disclaimers, are a marvel of radical melodic improvisation, or melodic phantasmagoria. It is music more various and strange—more beautiful—than is generally to be found in his later work, which is melodically barren and, let us say, strangled. And for that we may blame "high culture," something often fatal to jazz.

OTHERS

Al Haig is more contained, more stringent than George Wallington, has better taste, but Wallington, particularly in the early fifties, has more velocity and dramatic interest.

Lightness of touch versus billowing touch. Haig, the classic among boppers, displays a very significant development in texture from the fifties to the seventies. Wallington's sound, always brimming with spirit and wit, likewise evolves from a kind of clipped lush to something more soulful.

Dodo Marmarosa displays uncanny shading effects. But no monk in Marmarosa. An unerring melodic instinct sometimes leads him to sound like Rainbow Room jazz, though he never loses touch with the silence. Broken gorgeous.

Liquid sparkling Marmarosa.

No one faster or more relaxed than Joe Albany. This involves a certain sleight of hand and systematic truncation. He is always simultaneously lagging behind and overtaking himself. Elaborating the Tatum massive into an American baroque.

Joe Albany, in a recorded interview: what matters is not the hard life or easy living, but dedication to the music. This apropos of Charlie Parker, whose music is essentially "melodic," as the man is "humble before God." Albany's daughter suggests that his own playing was sometimes desperate.

Walter Bishop, Jr.: the bebop whirl drawn tight, instinctive bebop, very pure—as opposed to John Lewis's analytic bebop. Neither man develops.

You never hear him talked about (although he was much in demand as a sideman, from Dizzy to Rollins to Jackie McLean), but he is one of the subtlest and most rigorous colorists of the bebop piano: Wade Legge. A master in the art of slipping up quietly on yourself, while building a powerhouse, both fleet and soulful. Way out front. (His solo on "Little Niles," with Gigi Gryce's "Jazz Lab" in 1957, of real magnitude.)

Legge with Mingus in '57, at the end of his brief career: pushing conventions to the extreme, while remaining entirely pianistic. Illuminating, spiky lyricism, sound with an edge: melodic bop.

Two more melodists: Whereas twenty-year-old Gene Di Novi lags behind the beat, sizzling in the friction generated, Eddie Costa seems always to be waxing and ramifying in advance of the beat. What Nietzsche called the gift of melody is tied to a power of anticipation in recollection.

Strong if not assertive: Eddie Costa's piano. Darkly mirthful and often cheeky. When he first came on the scene, he was perceived as playing "modern swing"; now we can hear in his phrasing and accentuation an epitome of the evolving bop idiom.

There is a laid-back quality in the young Freddie Redd that is a little affected and that is outgrown in the playing of the older man.

Russ Freeman's piano is so resonant it sounds like a stringed instrument. Those church chords in all their rondeur laid back.

Jimmy Rowles: *the* jazz colorist.

In Phineas Newborn, Jr., velocity is pushed to the

point where the linear has become the planar, unfolding sheets of sound punctuated by droplets of color. *Refinement* of velocity into grace.

In bebop, melodic genius is allied to supersonic speed: Powell, Hope, Twardzik, Nichols, Marmarosa. Monk, the highest melodic genius of them all, is the most literally supersonic; the speed is *felt* but not heard as notes. They are all, in a crucial sense (gestural, if you like), working off the sound, and their music has this palpable physicality. After bebop, velocity tends to separate off from melody, though there are many exceptions.

As soon as jazz musicians were given the public recognition long denied them, and had shed their semi-criminal aura (I'm talking about the popular "rediscovery" of jazz in the early Seventies), the music stopped growing, if not living. "All the poisons necessary to the creation of masterpieces" (Baudelaire) were henceforth available only in places like Havana or Amsterdam.

Correction: It continued growing in the field of vocals—above all, with Betty Carter, Sheila Jordan, and Cassandra Wilson.

Rubalcaba: what pianist more exciting? More romantic? For all his former isolation, he has remained in touch with the contemporary hard-driving, McCoy Tyner-inspired piano style—though he is more brilliant, more wide-ranging, more delicate, above all more melodic than any of the (North) Americans in this bag. Witness the 1995 recording of "Perfidia." He has had to free himself from a certain rigorist imperative and a certain linearity, at the same time that he has risked, in his compositions, a certain saccharine quality reminiscent of Bill Evans in the Seventies (where the slide into schmalz is likewise signaled by recourse to electric piano or synthesizer): it is, in both respects, an ongoing struggle for him. But in the process he has given us a genuine reinterpretation of the modern jazz classics. And with his magnificent strummed sound, as of a harpsichord sometimes, and his deeply informed, highly refined technique, he has established a new standard for the mainstream.

Index

A

Adorno, Theodore 19, 82, 115
Agee, James 50, 53
A Kind of Loving 70
Albany, Joe 117
Another Year 74
A Page of Madness 38
Asphalt Jungle, The 53
Astaire, Fred 51, 103
A Taste of Honey 65
Austen, Jane 2, 4

B

Baby Doll 55-56
Beat Suite, The 94
beau Serge, Le 64
Beauty and the Beast (Cocteau) 41
Believers, The 71
Bicycle Thief, The 57-58, 65
Billy Liar 66, 71
Blonde Venus 39-40
Bremer, Louise 51
Bresson, Robert 59, 61
Burch, Noël 48, 76
Byard, Jaki 85, 86, 88

C

Camille 54
Capra, Frank 48
Carter, Betty 119
Cervantes, Miguel de 22
Cézanne, Paul 59, 99
Cherry, Don 93

Citizen Kane 49, 68
Cold Comfort Farm 69-70
Coleman, Ornette 83, 88
Coleridge, Samuel Taylor 5
Coltrane, John 86, 116
Costa, Eddie 118
Cousins, Les 64
Crowd, The 49
Curse of the Cat People 50

D

Davis, Miles 92, 103
Day of the Locust, The 71
Day of Wrath 44-45
Deleuze, Gilles 57
Descartes, René 8
De Sica, Vittorio 63, 65
Diary of a Country Priest 59-60
Dickens, Charles 4, 11, 51
Dietrich, Marlene 39, 40
Dolphy, Eric 79, 80-90, 94, 95
Dreier, Hans 55
Dreyer, Carl 42, 43, 47, 59, 75

E

Earth 37
8½ (Fellini) 67-69
Eisenstein, Sergei 38
Eldorado (L'Herbier) 35, 72
Elephant Man, The 72-73
Ellington, Duke 84, 93, 98, 102, 114
Epstein, Jean 35, 75
Evans, Bill 103, 120
Evans, Gil 93

F

Fall of the House of Usher (Epstein) *35, 72*
Far Cry 79, 85, 88
Faust (Murnau) *35*
Fosse, Bob 103

G

Gance, Abel 62
Garbo, Greta 54
Gaslight 50
Gertrud 42, 46, 47
Gillespie, Dizzy 91, 103, 106, 118
Great Expectations 11-15

H

Haig, Al 106, 117
Hamlet 5-10, 13, 14
Hope, Elmo 111, 119

I

Ikiru 62
I Remember Mama 53
It's a Wonderful Life 52

J

Jordan, Sheila 114, 119
Joyce, James 21, 22

K

Kafka, Franz 15, 16, 17, 18, 20, 21, 22, 23, 24, 81
Kant, Immanuel 2
Kazan, Elia 76
King Lear 8-11
Klee, Paul 99
Kurosawa, Akira 62

L

Lacy, Steve 85, 91-99, 103
L'Argent (Bresson) *61*
La Signora di Tutti *33, 48*
L'Atalante *33, 48*
L'Avventura *65*
Legge, Wade 118
Leigh, Mike 74
"Letter to His Father" 22
Levitt, Helen 53
Lewis, George 97, 117
L'Herbier, Marcel 35
L'Inhumaine *34-35, 72*
Little Foxes, The *49*
Lolita (Kubrick) *66*
Loring, Eugene 51
Lost Highway *72*
Lynch, David 72, 73

M

Maddin, Guy 73-74
Magnificent Ambersons, The *49*
Marmarosa, Dodo 117, 119
Master of the House *40*
Meantime *74*
Ménilmontant *38*
Michael *42-43, 45*
Mifune, Toshiro 63
Mingus, Charles 84, 86, 88, 89, 90, 93, 95, 110, 118
Miracle in Milan *59*
Mizoguchi, Kenji 56, 57
Molière, Jean Baptiste 2
Monk, Thelonious 86, 87, 91, 92, 96-99, 101-106, 108, 111, 112, 114, 115, 119
Morgan! *66*
Mouchette *61*
My Winnipeg *74*

N

Napoleon 38
Nichols, Herbie 104, 112-114, 119
Nietzsche, Friedrich 25, 118
Night and the City 54

O

Ophuls, Max 33
Ordet 45-46
Out to Lunch 86-88

P

Pabst, G. W. 71
Pandora's Box 37
Parker, Charlie 79-81, 83-89, 91, 103, 108-110, 117
Pather Panchali 63-64
Picasso, Pablo 22
Pierrot Lunaire 81, 82
Plato 8, 24
Powell, Bud 91, 98, 102, 106-109, 111, 116, 119
Pride and Prejudice 1-4

Q

Queen Kelly 35-37

R

Ray, Satyajit 61, 63
Renoir, Jean 48, 63
Roach, Max 90, 112
Rubalcaba, Gonzalo 119-120
Rudd, Roswell 96, 99, 113, 114
Russell, Pee Wee 84, 88, 97, 101

S

Same Old Song 70
Schoenberg, Arnold 22, 81, 82, 83, 98, 115
School Days 92, 96
Seastrom, Victor 63
Seitz, John 55
Shakespeare, William 2, 8
Sternberg, Josef von 39, 55
Stravinsky, Igor 97
Stroheim, Erich von 71
Sunrise 40, 86
Sunset Boulevard 54
Swanson, Gloria 54

T

Tati, Jacques 48
Tatum, Art 102, 103, 117
Taylor, Cecil 80, 90, 91, 95, 97, 98, 106, 109, 114-116
The Cabinet of Dr. Caligari 35
The Idiot (Kurosawa) 63
"The Metamorphosis" 24
The New Babylon 37-38
The Postmaster 61
The Quiet One 53
The Rules of the Game 42, 48
The Trial 22-23
"The Zürau Aphorisms" 15
Tolstoy, Leo 106
Twardzik, Dick 108-110, 119

U

Umberto D. 58-59, 66

V

Vampyr 43, 69
Vertov, Dziga 37
Vigo, Jean 33

W

Webern, Anton von 82, 98, 99
Welles, Orson 40
Wild Strawberries 68, 75
Wilson, Cassandra 119

Y

Yokihi 56
Yolanda and the Thief 51

Z

Zavattini, Cesare 59
Ziegfeld Follies 51

HOWARD EILAND is a critic and translator who grew up in the American South and Midwest, attending college and graduate school at a time when film societies abounded on campus and jazz was resurfacing on radio. He is the author, with Michael W. Jennings, of *Walter Benjamin: A Critical Life*.

www.ingramcontent.com/pod-product-compliance
Lightning Source LLC
Chambersburg PA
CBHW020140130526
44591CB00030B/163